MASTERING QUICKBOOKS ONLINE 2025

Effortless Payroll Solutions for Small, Medium, and Large Enterprises

TABLE OF CONTENT

TABLE OF CONTENT III

EMBRACE THE FUTURE WITH QUICKBOOKS ONLINE 2025 1

Adapt Now for a Smoother Tomorrow 4

W-2 Printing and Mailing Options 4

3. Go Green 5

1099 Form Printing and Mailing Options 5

1. Electronic Delivery 5

2. Paper Copies 5

Plan Ahead for Cost-Effective Compliance 5

MUST-HAVE TOOLS AND UPDATES IN QUICKBOOKS ONLINE 2025 6

SIMPLIFY YEAR-END BOOKKEEPING WITH QUICKBOOKS ONLINE 6

1. AUTO-CATEGORIZATION AND EXPENSE MANAGEMENT 6

How to Use Auto-Categorization: 7

2. Bank and Credit Card Reconciliation 7

Steps for Efficient Reconciliation: 7

3. Year-End Review with QuickBooks Reports 7

Profit and Loss Report: 7

Balance Sheet Report: 8

Trial Balance Report: 8

4. 1099 Tracking and E-Filing Options 8

How to Set Up 1099 Tracking: 8

5. Wrapping Up Accounts Receivable and Invoices 8

Steps for Year-End A/R Review: 8

6. Preparing Clients for 2025 with Cash Flow Projections 9

WHO THIS BOOK IS FOR 9

QUICKBOOKS ONLINE VS. DESKTOP 10

What is QuickBooks Used For? 10

Perfect for Beginners 10

Tailor It to Your Business 11

Collaboration Made Easy 11

Integration with Powerful Apps 11

High-Level Data Security 12

Affordable Pricing Options 12

Mobile App for On-the-Go Management.. 12
Fast and Reliable Customer Support... 12
Scalable for Business Growth.. 12
Final Thoughts.. 12

CHAPTER 1 .... **13**

GETTING STARTED WITH QUICKBOOKS ONLINE **13**

QUICK START CHECKLIST.. 13
1. Get Familiar with the Dashboard... 13
2. Enter Your Company Details.. 13
3. Set Up Sales Preferences.. 13
4. Import Your Business Data... 14
5. Link Your Bank Accounts and Credit Cards.. 14
6. Payroll Software Integration.. 14
7. Add Necessary Integrations.. 14
8. Set Up Tax Preferences.. 14
The QuickBooks Online Business View: A Smarter Way to Manage Your Data........ 15
1. Setting Up the Dashboard.. 15
2. Entering Your Company Details... 15
3. Sales Settings Setup.. 15
4. Import Your Business Data... 16
5. Link Your Bank Accounts.. 17
6. Integrate Payroll Software.. 17
7. Add Other Integrations.. 17
8. Get Ready for Tax Season.. 17
Simplify Tax Season with QuickBooks Payroll... 18
How to Reconcile in QuickBooks Online... 18
3. Check the Audit History... 19
How to Undo Reconciliation in QuickBooks Online... 19
Adding an Accountant to Undo Reconciliation 19
Manually Undo Reconciliation 20
HOW TO DELETE A DEPOSIT IN QUICKBOOKS ONLINE.. 20
QuickBooks Online Alternatives.. 21
WHAT'S NEW IN QUICKBOOKS ONLINE 2025 21
Internet Speed and Browser Compatibility 21
Internet and Display:... 22

Printing:..22

Supported Browsers for Windows: 23

Supported Browsers for macOS: 23

FREQUENTLY ASKED QUESTIONS 23

Surface / Windows 8 Devices:...................................24

GETTING STARTED WITH QUICKBOOKS ONLINE 25

Welcome to QuickBooks Online!................................25

Minute 1: Align QuickBooks Online with Real-Life Transactions 26

Minute 2: Set Up Your Company Information.............26

Minute 4: Set Your Fiscal Year Start Date 28

Minute 5: Choose Your Accounting Method: Cash or Accrual 29

Minute 6: Set Your Accounting Currency 29

Minute 7: Upload Your Company Logo 30

Minute 8: Set Default Invoice Payment Terms...........31

Minute 9: Set Up Sales Tax..31

Minute 12: QuickBooks Test Drive - Practice Creating an Invoice 32

Why Test Drive is Valuable..33

Take a Moment to Reflect on Your Goals 34

Navigation Menu Overview 35

Understanding Your QuickBooks Online Navigation Menu 36

Customizing Your Navigation Menu 37

Bookmarking Pages in QuickBooks Online................37

To remove a bookmark: 37

To hide or show a page:..37

Additional Resources 38

Key Takeaways:..38

Step 1: Sign Up and Choose the Right Plan...............39

Step 2: Customize Your Settings...............................40

Step 3: Link Your Bank and Credit Card Accounts ...40

Step 4: Organize Your Chart of Accounts 40

Step 5: Enter Opening Balances 40

Step 6: Invite Your Accountant..................................40

Make Your Dashboard Work for You 41

Create Custom Reports 41

Integrate Third-Party Apps 41

AUTOMATING FOR EFFICIENCY..............................41

Customizable Reports 42

Track Financial Performance in Real Time 42

Analyze Spending and Expenses 42

CHAPTER 2 .... **44**

MASTERING FINANCIAL BASICS **44**

Streamline Your Finances with QuickBooks Online 2025 44

Your Road to Mastery 47

Core Features: Invoices, Expenses, and Sales 47

Setting Up the Chart of Accounts in QuickBooks Online 52

How to Add a New Account to Your Chart of Accounts 54

Step 3: Save Your New Account 56

Simplifying Your QuickBooks Online Chart Accounts with flye 57

1. Automatic Account Import 57

2. Comprehensive Account Mapping 57

3. Simplified Account Naming 58

4. Custom Product and Service Mapping 58

5. Integration of Classes, Departments, and Projects 58

6. Control Over Account Mappings 58

7. Auto-Sync for Updates 58

Step 1: Access the Chart of Accounts 58

Step 2: Deactivate the Account 59

Step 3: Confirm Deactivation 60

1. Sign In to QuickBooks Online 61

2. Access the Banking Section 61

3. Add a Bank Account 61

4. Search for Your Bank 61

5. Enter Your Login Credentials 61

6. Complete Authentication 61

7. Choose Accounts to Connect 61

8. Review and Confirm 61

9. Categorize Transactions 62

10. Reconcile Your Account 62

HOW TO CONNECT CREDIT CARD ACCOUNTS TO QUICKBOOKS ONLINE 62

Step-by-Step Process 62

Conclusion 63

Key Takeaways 64

Benefits of Accounting Automation 65

Stay Compliant 66

Save Money 66

Reconciliation 67

Expense Management 67

Expense Management 68

Reporting and Analytics 68

Forecasting 68

Financial Forecasting 69

Accounts Receivable and Accounts Payable 69

Tax Management 70

CHAPTER 3 71

STREAMLINING INVOICING AND PAYMENTS 71

Top E-Invoicing Trends for 2025 71

1. AI and Machine Learning Leading the Way 71

2. Blockchain Ensuring Security and Transparency 72

3. Growing Adoption of Cloud-Based Solutions 72

4. Enhanced Interoperability and Standardization 72

5. Focus on Sustainability 73

CREATING AND CUSTOMIZING PROFESSIONAL INVOICES 73

Why You Should Customize Your Invoices 73

Customizing your invoices in QuickBooks Online allows you to: 73

How to Get Started with Custom Invoices 74

What is QuickBooks Online? 74

Why Customized Invoices Matter 74

1. Increase Brand Visibility 74

2. Add a Personal Touch 75

Add a Personal Touch 75

Here are some ideas: 75

The Benefits: 76

Steps for QuickBooks Online Users 77

Here's how to get started: 77

Customizing Invoices in QuickBooks Online 78

How to Customize an Invoice Template in QuickBooks Desktop 78

This opens a customization window where you can:.. 78

Setting Up Recurring Invoices in QuickBooks Online 79

Set Up Invoice Payment Settings: 81

Updating Payment Options on Invoices... 81

Optional: To email the invoice: 81

For the New Invoicing System 81

Optional: To send the invoice via email: 82

Processing Sales Receipts for Payments 82

Printing Receipts 83

2. Ensure Your Invoice is Clear and Comprehensive.. 84

3. Set Up a Follow-Up System for Overdue Payments 85

Benefits of accounting software: 85

Step 2: Review Your Sales Tax Liability 88

Step 4: Verify Payment and Save Records 89

Step 5: Automate Sales Tax Management with TaxCloud................................... 89

CHAPTER 4 .... **90**

MANAGING EXPENSES AND BILLS **90**

Step 1: Sign In to Your Account 90

Step 2: Navigate the Bills Page 90

Recording Bill Payments... 91

RECORDING EXPENSES AND UPLOADING RECEIPTS IN A SNAP.............................. 91

Before You Start 92

Upload Receipts or Bills from Your Computer.. 93

Snap a Photo of Receipts or Bills with Your Mobile Device............................... 93

Step-by-Step Guide:.. 94

Email Receipts or Bills to QuickBooks 94

Step 2: Review, Add, or Match Receipts and Bills 94

On a Web Browser 95

1. Access Receipts 95

2. Review the "For Review" Tab 95

3. Take Action Based on Matches 95

4. Track Reviewed Items 96

Keep Your Records Accurate 96

Paying Vendors with QuickBooks: Online and Desktop 97

Key Steps for Vendor Payments 97

How to Pay Vendors in QuickBooks Online 98

Enhance Vendor Payments with Third-Party Apps 98

Selecting the Delivery Method 99

If You Choose to Pay by Check 100

Important Notes 100

Scheduling Recurring Bills to Stay Ahead of Deadlines 102

What Can You Automate? 102

Completing the Details for a Recurring Template 105

1. Template Name 105

2. Transaction Type 105

3. Interval 105

4. Start Date 105

5. End Options 105

6. Template Body 105

7. Save Template 106

Managing Recurring Transactions 106

Tracking Business Expenses for Tax Deductions 106

CHAPTER 5 .... **107**

PAYROLL AND EMPLOYEE MANAGEMENT MADE SIMPLE **107**

Integrating Factorial with QuickBooks 107

Key Features of QuickBooks Payroll Online: 109

2. Tax Filing 110

4. Employee Self-Service 110

1. Simplified HR Management 111

2. Employee Self-Service Portal 111

3. Time and Attendance Tracking 111

4. Streamlined Recruitment and Onboarding 111

6. Insights and Analytics 111

7. Seamless Integrations 111

8. Scalable for All Business Sizes 111

The Power of Combining QuickBooks and Factorial 112

What Is Payroll Automation? 112

Payroll Tasks You Can Automate 113

How to Choose an Automated Payroll System 114

How to Connect QuickBooks and Unrubble 115

Steps to Connect QuickBooks and Unrubble 116

Why Integrate QuickBooks Time with Unrubble? 117

MANAGING BENEFITS BONUSES AND CONTRACTOR PAYMENTS 119

Independent Contractor vs. Employee: Understanding the IRS Distinction 119

Setting Up Contractor Records in QuickBooks Online 120

1. Collect Form W-9 120

2. Add Them as Vendors 120

3. Record Payments 120

Paying Independent Contractors 121

CHAPTER 6 122

REAL TIME FINANCIAL REPORTING 122

Key Features and Benefits of Real-Time Accounting and Financial Reporting 122

Improved Decision-Making 123

Better Cash Flow Management 124

Greater Accuracy and Transparency 124

The Role of Cloud Technology 124

Remote Access 124

Real-Time Collaboration 125

High-Level Security 125

The Future of Real-Time Accounting 125

Artificial Intelligence and Machine Learning 125

Advanced Analytics Capabilities 125

Greater Integration 126

Conclusion 126

UNLOCKING THE POWER OF QUICKBOOKS REPORTS 126

TYPES OF REPORTS IN QUICKBOOKS 126

1. Financial Reports 126

2. Inventory Reports 126

3. Customer and Vendor Reports 127

4. Job Status Reports 127

Easily Share Financial Data with Your Team 130

Clarity for Tax Planning and Beyond 130

What Are QuickBooks Dashboards? 131

1. Visual Representations of Financial Data 131

2. Performance Tracking 131

3. Customization Options 131

SPOTTING TRENDS AND OPPORTUNITIES FOR GROWTH 133

Who Is QuickBooks For? 133

Custom Solutions for Diverse Needs 133

Marketing Approach 134

MARKETING STRATEGIES THAT DRIVE QUICKBOOKS' SUCCESS 135

Content Marketing 135

Strategic Partnerships 135

Customer Support and Training 135

Innovation and Data-Driven Insights 135

Building Authority and Engagement 136

Further engagement is driven through: 136

A Holistic Approach 136

CHAPTER 7 137

TAX SEASON SIMPLIFIED 137

1. Expense Management with Auto-Categorization 137

2. Bank and Credit Card Reconciliation 137

Steps for Reconciliation: 137

3. Year-End Reports 137

4. 1099 Tracking and E-Filing 138

5. Accounts Receivable and Invoice Management 138

6. Cash Flow Projections for 2025 138

Streamline Your Year-End Tasks with QuickBooks Online 139

What Is Prep for Taxes? 139

Key Features to Optimize Tax Preparation 139

5. Snapshot of Income and Expenses 140

6. Better Organization and Categorization 140

7. Improved Client Communication 140

8. Efficient Review and Editing 140

Preparing for Success in Tax Season 141

Generating Tax Reports to Hand Off to Your Accountant 141

Navigating Tax Changes and Avoiding Filing Mistakes 143

Mistake 1: Misreporting Income 143

Corporate Tax Challenges 144

Key Business Credits: 145

Tax Information Errors 145

Late Payment Penalties 146

For Individuals: 146

For Businesses: 146

Outdated Records 147

CHAPTER 8 148

ADVANCED FEATURES FOR GROWING BUSINESSES 148

How QuickBooks Can Transform Your HVAC Business 148

Why QuickBooks is Perfect for HVAC Businesses 148

Here's how QuickBooks simplifies financial management: 148

1. Streamlined Invoicing 150

2. Job Cost Tracking 150

3. Simplified Payroll 150

4. Inventory Management 150

5. Custom Reports 150

Why QuickBooks is a Smart Choice for HVAC Businesses 151

Choosing the Right QuickBooks Version for Your HVAC Business 151

Benefits of Inventory Tracking with QuickBooks Online 151

Choosing the Right Inventory Tracking Solution 152

Key Features of QuickBooks Online Inventory Management 153

What Items Can You Track with QuickBooks Online? 154

Maximizing QuickBooks Online Inventory Management 154

How QuickBooks Online Inventory Tracking Can Help You and Limitations 155

How to Set Up QuickBooks Online Inventory Tracking 156

Step 1: Enable Inventory Tracking 156

Step 2: Add Your Inventory Products 156

Step 3: Track What Sells 158

Step 4: Restock Your Inventory 158

Step 5: Use Reports to Monitor Inventory 158

Multi-Currency Transactions for Global Businesses 159

Enabling Multicurrency in QuickBooks 159

How to Turn On Multicurrency in QuickBooks Online 160

Adding Currencies in QuickBooks Online 160

Deleting Currencies in QuickBooks Online 160

Which Record Types Does QuickBooks Multicurrency Support? 161

Enhance QuickBooks Multicurrency with Add-On Integrations...........................161

Key Features of Tipalti Integration 161

Benefits of Streamlining Global Payables 162

Tipalti Multi-FX Benefits for Currency Conversion and Payments 162

CHAPTER 9 163

TROUBLESHOOTING AND SUPPORT 163

Initial Troubleshooting Steps 163

User Troubleshooting Tips 163

System-Related Issues to Consider..164

Browser 164

Computer 164

Network...164

Printer 164

Data Entry Troubleshooting..164

Report Issues 165

Common Causes of Login Problems with QuickBooks Online 165

How to Fix It 168

How to Fix It 168

QuickBooks Won't Open Error 168

How to Fix QuickBooks Not Opening Error 169

How to Resolve It 170

Lost or No Connection to Data Files..170

Steps to Troubleshoot QuickBooks Network and File Access Issues 171

How to Fix Error H202 171

Common User Questions and Fixes...171

How to Get Help..172

Why Contact QuickBooks Support? 172

How to Reach QuickBooks Desktop Enterprise Support 173

Tips for a Better Experience: 173

Steps to Start a Live Chat: 173

3. Submit an Online Support Request 174

4. QuickBooks Community 174

5. Social Media Support 174

Tips for a Smooth Support Experience 174

Additional Support Resources 175

Backing Up Your Data for Peace of Mind..175

Data you can backup..176

What You Can't Restore from a QuickBooks Backup......................................176

1. Budgets 176

2. Stock Details...176

3. VAT Rates (Expense Accounts)...176

4. Personal Cloud Archive Data 177

MANAGING BACKUPS IN QUICKBOOKS..177

CHAPTER 10 ....**179**

QUICKBOOKS ONLINE FOR ENTREPRENEURS AND BEYOND **179**

Why Switch to QuickBooks Online? 179

Future-Proof Your Accounting with QuickBooks Online 180

1. AI and Machine Learning Take the Lead..181

2. Blockchain for Secure and Transparent Transactions..............................181

4. Push for Interoperability and Standardization......................................182

5. Sustainability Takes the Spotlight 182

4. Digital Identity Verification 182

5. International Cooperation Among Tax Authorities..................................183

Why Best Practices Are Essential 184

QuickBooks Online Tips for Business Owners 184

The Bottom Line 185

The Future of Cloud Accounting with QuickBooks Online in 2025..................185

Get a Real-Time Snapshot of Your Business...186

Easy Cloud-Based Collaboration 187

Simplified QuickBooks Year-End Tips for Business Owners and Accountants 187

1. Auto-Categorization for Expenses...188

2. Bank and Credit Card Reconciliation..188

3. QuickBooks Reports for Year-End Review 188

4. 1099 Tracking and Filing 189

5. Accounts Receivable (A/R) Management 189

6. Cash Flow Projections for 2025..189

INDEX..**190**

EMBRACE THE FUTURE WITH QUICKBOOKS ONLINE 2025

We're thrilled to announce Intuit QuickBooks as a key partner for the launch of our Festival of Accounting & Bookkeeping (FAB). Recognized globally as a leader in online accounting solutions for accountants, bookkeepers, small businesses, and the self-employed, QuickBooks is the ideal collaborator to help us kick off this groundbreaking event.

Over the years, our collaboration with Intuit QuickBooks has grown, including their role as the lead sponsor of the Accounting Excellence Awards. Now, we're teaming up once again to bring a fresh, innovative experience to accounting professionals across the Midlands and beyond.

QuickBooks has consistently prioritized empowering accountants, bookkeepers, and their clients with tools that truly make a difference. At FAB, you'll witness this dedication firsthand with actionable insights and practical strategies that you can apply directly to your practice.

As a launch partner, Intuit QuickBooks will deliver dynamic sessions featuring product updates, expert tips, and forward-thinking strategies. These presentations will demonstrate how to enhance your service offerings, better support your clients, and scale your practice with confidence.

QuickBooks stands out for its smart, intuitive accounting and bookkeeping software, which saves time and money while offering a seamless experience for users. With options ranging from QuickBooks Simple Start to QuickBooks Advanced, businesses of all sizes and industries can find a solution tailored to their needs. Trusted by over 6.5 million subscribers worldwide, QuickBooks offers unparalleled reliability and simplicity.

During the festival, you'll have the opportunity to explore their cutting-edge technology and connect with their team to learn about:

- Helping your clients save on software licenses.
- Gaining access to free accounting and payroll software for your practice.
- Utilizing advanced practice management tools to cater to diverse client needs.

Mark your calendar for 13-14 March 2024, and join us at The NEC Birmingham for this one-of-a-kind event! Expect a mix of insightful sessions, hands-on experiences, and plenty of fun along the way.

Don't miss out—sign up for our newsletter to stay updated on FAB news. If you're interested in becoming an exhibitor, reach out and secure your spot at this revolutionary festival.

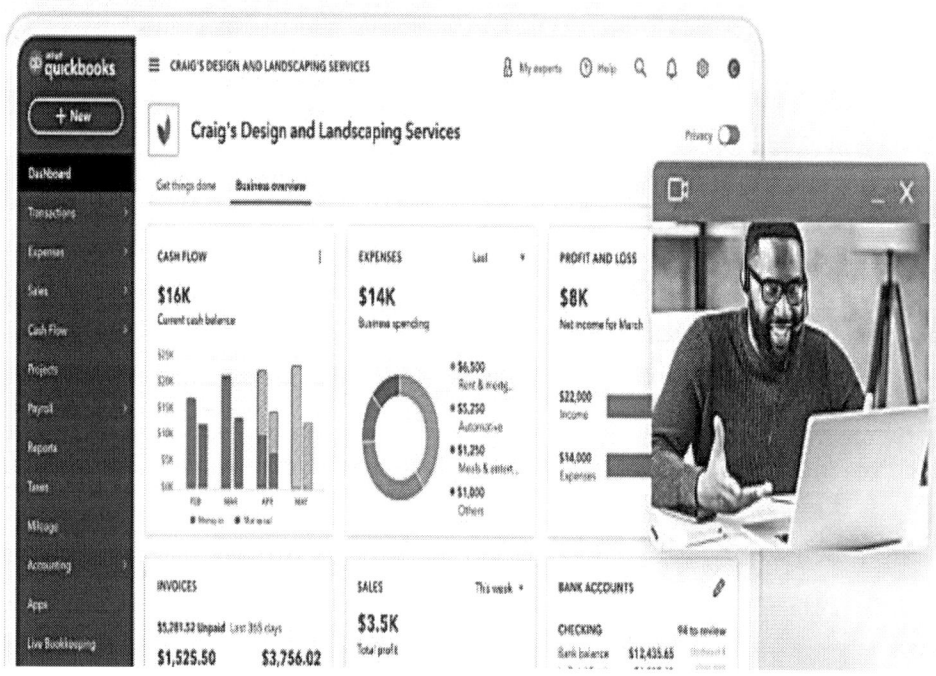

EMBRACING THE FUTURE OF BUSINESS ACCOUNTING

As we approach the quarter-century mark of the 21st century, financial management tools are evolving to meet the demands of modern businesses. Intuit has announced major updates to its QuickBooks Desktop suite, signaling a shift towards innovative, cloud-based solutions. Starting May 31, 2025, all versions of QuickBooks Desktop 2022—including Pro, Premier, Mac, and Enterprise Solutions v22—will be discontinued.

If your business relies on these tools, now is the time to adapt to avoid disruptions. Transitioning to QuickBooks Online (QBO) not only ensures continuity but also brings enhanced efficiency, improved collaboration, and unmatched flexibility—ideal for today's fast-paced business world.

WHY MAKE THE SWITCH TO QUICKBOOKS ONLINE?

1. User-Friendly Design

QuickBooks Online is built for simplicity, making it easy to navigate even for non-technical users. If you're already familiar with QuickBooks Desktop, the transition will be seamless, thanks to its intuitive interface and familiar features.

2. Enhanced Team Collaboration

Unlike Desktop versions, QBO allows multiple users to access the system simultaneously without requiring additional licenses. This fosters seamless collaboration between team members and accountants, whether they're working in-office or remotely.

3. Anywhere, Anytime Access

As a cloud-based platform, QBO ensures you can access your financial data from any device—desktop, laptop, tablet, or smartphone. Whether managing inventory at a trade show or reviewing expenses on the go, QBO keeps you connected no matter where you are.

4. Effortless Maintenance

Say goodbye to installing updates, managing local data, or dealing with compatibility issues. With QBO, Intuit takes care of updates and system maintenance, allowing you to focus on running your business. Training your team is also easier, as QBO is accessible from anywhere with an internet connection.

5. Powerful Reporting and Insights

QBO's advanced reporting tools give you deeper insights into your business's financial health. Customizable dashboards and reports help you track key performance indicators, enabling smarter decisions to optimize costs and grow your business.

6. Streamlined Automation

QuickBooks Online automates routine tasks like invoicing and expense tracking, reducing the risk of errors while saving time. These features let you focus on strategic initiatives rather than repetitive administrative processes.

WHAT ABOUT QUICKBOOKS DESKTOP ENTERPRISE?

For businesses still using QuickBooks Desktop Enterprise, subscriptions for Enterprise 24.0 remain available beyond September 30, 2024, and existing customers can renew without interruptions. While Enterprise may suit companies that prefer desktop solutions, the future of this software is uncertain as the industry continues to pivot towards cloud-based tools.

Adapt Now for a Smoother Tomorrow

Switching to QuickBooks Online is more than just a software upgrade—it's a step toward embracing the future of business accounting. Don't wait until it's too late—start planning your transition today and unlock a world of smarter, faster, and more flexible financial management.

FUTURE-PROOF YOUR BUSINESS WITH QUICKBOOKS ONLINE

Intuit's move away from QuickBooks Desktop underscores the growing trend toward cloud-based solutions. QuickBooks Online (QBO) is designed to meet the demands of today's businesses with its ease of use, accessibility, and workflow automation. By transitioning to QBO, you'll not only secure your accounting processes but also unlock tools that enhance collaboration, improve reporting, and automate routine tasks.

Need help navigating the transition? Our team is ready to assist, ensuring your business stays ahead of the curve.

WHY QUICKBOOKS ONLINE 2025 IS A GAME-CHANGER

Important Updates for Printing and Mailing W-2 and 1099 Forms in 2025

Starting January 2025, for the 2024 tax season, QBO will introduce an additional fee of $4 per employee or vendor for printing and mailing W-2 and 1099 forms. This fee is separate from your current Payroll or Contractor Payments subscription.

W-2 Printing and Mailing Options

If you currently use automatic payroll report filings in QBO and want to avoid the additional fee, you'll need to adjust your approach. Here's what you can do:

1. Update Payroll Settings

Disable the automatic W-2 printing and mailing feature in your Payroll Settings by January 3, 2025.

2. Print and Mail Yourself

If you opt out of the QBO service, you can print and mail W-2 forms to employees manually.

3. Go Green

Encourage your employees to switch to paperless W-2s through QuickBooks Workforce, eliminating the need for printed copies entirely.

1099 Form Printing and Mailing Options

When finalizing 1099s in QBO, you'll need to decide how to distribute these forms to your vendors or contractors. Options include:

1. Electronic Delivery

If the vendor or contractor has an email address saved in QBO, the system can send the 1099 form electronically.

2. Paper Copies

If a vendor or contractor hasn't provided written consent for paperless delivery, the law requires you to provide a physical copy. You can either:

- Print and mail it yourself, or
- Use QBO's printing and mailing service for $4 per form.

Plan Ahead for Cost-Effective Compliance

By preparing in advance, you can choose the most convenient and budget-friendly method for managing your W-2 and 1099 forms while staying compliant with tax regulations. Whether you go paperless or handle the process yourself, QBO provides the tools you need to streamline your tax season efficiently.

MUST-HAVE TOOLS AND UPDATES IN QUICKBOOKS ONLINE 2025

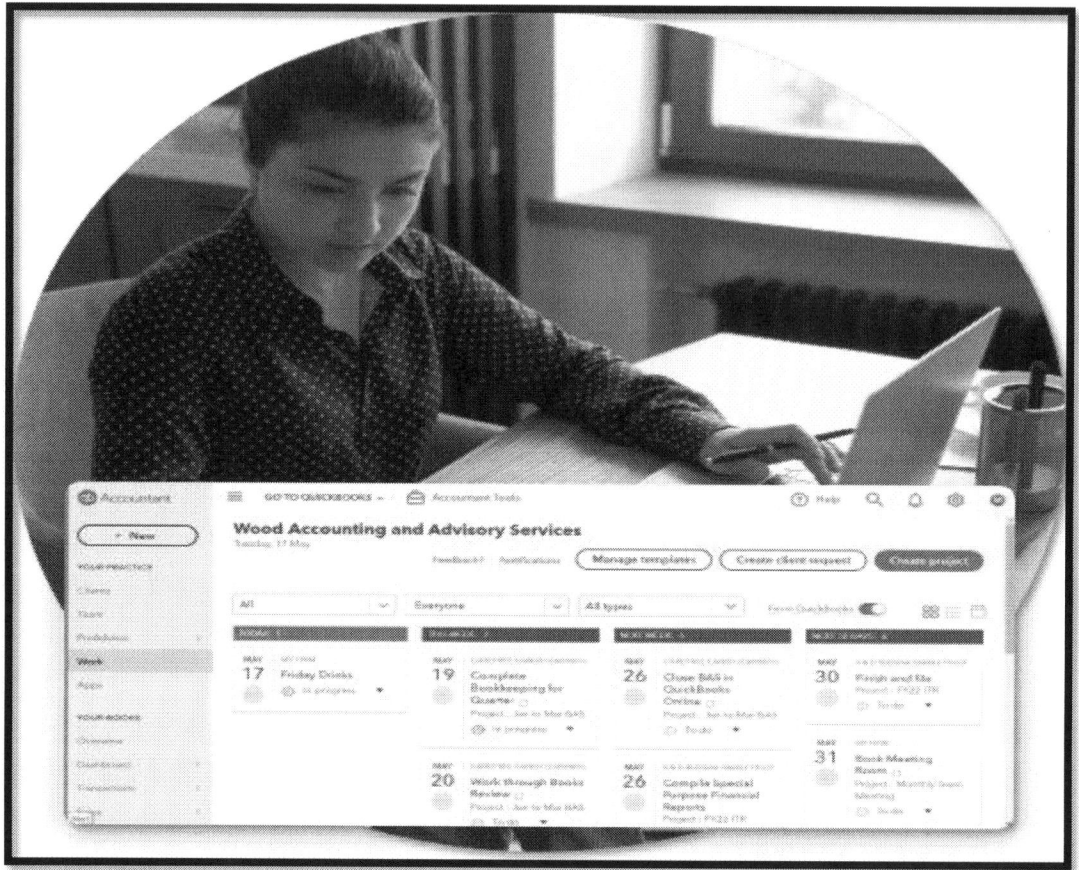

SIMPLIFY YEAR-END BOOKKEEPING WITH QUICKBOOKS ONLINE

As the year comes to a close, accountants and business owners gear up to finalize their books and prepare for the upcoming tax season. QuickBooks Online (QBO) offers a suite of features to streamline year-end tasks, ensuring your books are ready for 2025. From running detailed reports to managing expenses efficiently, here's how QBO makes year-end processing easier:

1. AUTO-CATEGORIZATION AND EXPENSE MANAGEMENT

Key Feature: Enhanced Auto-Categorization

QBO's advanced auto-categorization feature saves valuable time by automatically sorting recurring transactions. With rule-based tools, accountants can ensure transactions are assigned to the correct tax categories, making reconciliation a breeze.

How to Use Auto-Categorization:

- Set up or modify rules by navigating to Banking > Rules on the left sidebar.

- Define criteria based on vendor names or specific keywords to automatically categorize transactions.
- Review categorized transactions by selecting Banking > Categorize to spot and correct any discrepancies before finalizing expenses.

2. Bank and Credit Card Reconciliation

QBO's improved reconciliation feature ensures greater accuracy, helping you match transactions to bank statements quickly. This is particularly beneficial for businesses managing high transaction volumes.

Steps for Efficient Reconciliation:

- Go to Accounting > Reconcile, then select the account to reconcile. Enter the ending balance from the most recent statement.
- Use advanced filters to locate older, unreconciled transactions. QBO now alerts you about missing bank feeds to minimize errors.
- Mark transactions as reconciled by checking their boxes. Confirm the Difference column reads "0" to ensure everything balances correctly.

Reconciliation ensures that your QBO records match bank accounts, a critical step before filing taxes.

3. Year-End Review with QuickBooks Reports

QBO simplifies year-end reviews with customizable reports tailored to each client's needs. These reports offer quick insights into financial performance and identify areas needing adjustments.

ESSENTIAL YEAR-END REPORTS TO RUN

Profit and Loss Report:

Navigate to Reports > Profit & Loss to review income and expenses. Customize date ranges and focus on specific accounts for detailed analysis.

Balance Sheet Report:

Found under Reports > Balance Sheet, this report highlights assets versus liabilities, helping identify discrepancies.

Trial Balance Report:

Available at Reports > Accountant Reports, this report provides a snapshot of debits and credits across accounts, ensuring everything balances correctly.

By leveraging these tools and features, you can close out your books with confidence, making tax season preparation smoother and more efficient.

QBO allows you to filter reports by class or location, enabling more detailed insight into your business, thereby making your year-end review faster and more comprehensive.

4. 1099 Tracking and E-Filing Options

Simplified 1099-NEC & 1099-MISC Tracking

QuickBooks Online streamlines 1099 preparation by tracking contractor payments and offering automatic e-filing options. This ensures you stay organized with independent contractor expenses.

How to Set Up 1099 Tracking:

Navigate to Expenses > Vendors, create new vendors, or edit existing ones, ensuring you check the box for Track payments for 1099.

At the start of January, go to Expenses > Vendors > Prepare 1099s to identify vendors without a W-9 form and confirm their address details.

5. Wrapping Up Accounts Receivable and Invoices

Batch Invoice and A/R Management

QuickBooks' enhanced batch invoicing makes it easier for tax professionals to assist clients in finalizing accounts receivable (A/R) at year-end. Reviewing unbilled invoices and bad debts ensures accurate taxable income.

Steps for Year-End A/R Review:

Navigate to Sales > Invoices and generate the Open Invoices Report to identify outstanding amounts.

Use batch invoicing under Sales > Customers to select multiple clients or invoices and quickly apply payments or close out invoices using the batch action tool.

Generate the Accounts Receivable Aging Report under Reports > Accountant Reports to locate overdue accounts. These may need to be written off before year-end.

Addressing unpaid invoices ensures accurate year-end reporting and smooth book closure.

6. Preparing Clients for 2025 with Cash Flow Projections

QuickBooks' cash flow forecasting tool helps tax professionals provide clients with financial insights for the upcoming year. Available on Essentials and Plus plans, this tool offers regular updates to help clients evaluate their financial position heading into 2025.

How to Use Cash Flow Projections:

Go to Dashboard > Business Overview > Cash Flow to set up projections based on average monthly income and expenses.

Encourage clients to adjust projections for significant changes, such as major expenses or seasonal income variations.

Review the cash flow summary to estimate cash availability during the first quarter of 2025, helping client's budget and allocate funds effectively.

Clear cash flow insights allow clients to plan proactively and make informed financial decisions as they approach tax season.

WHO THIS BOOK IS FOR

QuickBooks Online is a cloud-based service. It allows you to get to your accounting software anywhere, as long as there is an internet connection where you are. You log in and manage your account with any device.

Cloud-based, QuickBooks Online itself backs up your data into their servers at Intuit without any need for physical storage space such as with the desktop version.

QUICKBOOKS ONLINE VS. DESKTOP

Which Should You Choose?

QuickBooks Desktop operates as traditional software installed on your computer, while QuickBooks Online offers cloud-based access to your data anytime, anywhere. This makes QuickBooks Online the more flexible option for many users.

What is QuickBooks Used For?

QuickBooks offers comprehensive finance and accounting tools, making it a go-to solution for small-to-medium-sized business owners. It helps streamline managing income, expenses, and overall financial tracking.

ACCESS ANYTIME, ANYWHERE WITH QUICKBOOKS ONLINE

With QuickBooks Online, your financial data is available wherever you are—at the office, at home, or on the move. Simply log in to manage your finances seamlessly.

- Flexibility for All: Business owners can stay updated on their books in real time, and accountants can work remotely. This accessibility makes QuickBooks Online far superior in convenience compared to its desktop version.

Perfect for Beginners

QuickBooks Online is user-friendly and intuitive, making it a great choice for beginners or those without a deep accounting background.

- **Ideal for Small Businesses:** It's an excellent tool for sole proprietors and small business owners to track income and expenses.
- **Scalable Solution**: As your business grows or your financial needs become more complex, QuickBooks Online can accommodate an accountant's input with ease.

Tailor It to Your Business

QuickBooks Online allows you to customize your account to suit your business needs.

Professional Customization: Add your company logo and details to invoices, sales receipts, and estimates to generate polished documents with just a few clicks.

AUTOMATION TO SAVE TIME

One of the standout features of QuickBooks Online is its time-saving automation capabilities.

Automate repetitive tasks like data entry, bank reconciliations, and bill payments, freeing up time to focus on growing your business.

QuickBooks Online isn't just accounting software—it's a powerful tool designed to simplify financial management and adapt to your business's evolving needs.

This saves a lot of time from manual work, which you can utilize in growing your business. If set up correctly, transactions become a breeze to review, hence streamlining the accounting process.

Collaboration Made Easy

QuickBooks Online makes teamwork effortless by allowing multiple users to work on the same financial data simultaneously. Sharing reports with your team or accountant is simple, and you can access the system from any device while on the go. If you're accustomed to desktop accounting software, switching to the cloud will revolutionize the way you work.

Integration with Powerful Apps

Think QuickBooks needs a boost? No problem. It integrates with thousands of apps that focus on specific tasks like expense tracking, inventory management, and timekeeping. For example, by connecting with Expensify, employees can easily scan receipts directly into QuickBooks, making expense reporting seamless and hassle-free.

High-Level Data Security

Your financial data is in safe hands with QuickBooks Online. The platform uses top-tier encryption and performs daily backups to protect your information. Intuit prioritizes security, so you can focus on your business without worrying about data breaches.

Affordable Pricing Options

QuickBooks Online offers multiple subscription tiers to suit your budget and business needs. Plans include Simple Start, Essentials, and Plus, with the option to save money through annual payments. Compared to alternatives like FreshBooks or Xero, QuickBooks Online is a cost-effective solution for small businesses.

Mobile App for On-the-Go Management

Stay connected to your finances wherever you are with the QuickBooks Online mobile app. From your smartphone or tablet, you can create invoices, track expenses, and access reports—whether you're on the road, at home, or in the office.

Fast and Reliable Customer Support

QuickBooks Online provides excellent customer support through live chat, phone assistance, and an extensive knowledge base. Whenever you need help, support is just a click or call away, with minimal wait times during business hours.

Scalable for Business Growth

QuickBooks Online is built to grow with your business. You can add users, upgrade your plan, and access new features as your needs evolve—all without overpaying for services you don't use. Whether you're a solo entrepreneur or managing a growing team, QuickBooks offers flexibility to match your business's changing demands.

Final Thoughts

QuickBooks Online offers a wide range of benefits for businesses of all sizes. From payroll management to customizable reports, its features simplify financial management at every level. Whether you're a solopreneur or running a larger operation, QuickBooks Online is a tool worth trying. With its flexibility, affordability, and robust features, it could be the game-changer your business needs.

CHAPTER 1

GETTING STARTED WITH QUICKBOOKS ONLINE

QuickBooks Online is arguably the best accounting software solution, an immediate choice for nearly any business, and it outcompetes other highly-rated options, including FreshBooks and Zoho Books, in comprehensive research tests. If you're new to the software, take some time to get familiar with how QuickBooks works. If you're in a very specialized business sector, such as hospitality, you may want to take a closer look at industry-specific choices to make certain that the needs of your operation are well-covered.

The following guide will take you through the necessary steps involved in setting up QuickBooks Online for your business. From reconciling accounts to managing deposits, this tutorial covers the very basics and offers helpful tips along the way.

All businesses have some accounting to do, and it's essential to know what features, pricing plans, and support options to focus on. Once you have finished reading this tutorial, you will be able to move confidently within QuickBooks Online and find what you need in a snap. Pro Tip: While filling out any form, remember to hit Alt + S to save - fast and easy!

QUICK START CHECKLIST

Getting started with QuickBooks Online is easier than you think. Here's how you can set up your business in a few easy steps:

1. Get Familiar with the Dashboard

Spend time exploring the interface to understand where essential tools and features are located.

2. Enter Your Company Details

Business information, like the name of the company, address, and contact, can be put in for personalization.

3. Set Up Sales Preferences

Invoicing, payment terms, discounts, etc., can be set up here as per your business requirement.

4. Import Your Business Data

Set up your existing records in QuickBooks Online, such as customer lists and product inventory.

5. Link Your Bank Accounts and Credit Cards

Link your bank accounts with QuickBooks to make tracking and reconciling easier.

6. Payroll Software Integration

If you have a payroll service, integrate it with QuickBooks for ease of paying your employees.

7. Add Necessary Integrations

Enhance your setup by connecting apps that improve functionality, like inventory management or expense tracking tools.

8. Set Up Tax Preferences

Configure tax settings, including sales tax rates and filing preferences, to ensure compliance.

This checklist will bring you up and running with QuickBooks Online. Whether you are a new user or a migrated user from any other platform, QuickBooks makes accounting easy for businesses of all sizes. Take a plunge and make managing your books a piece of cake!

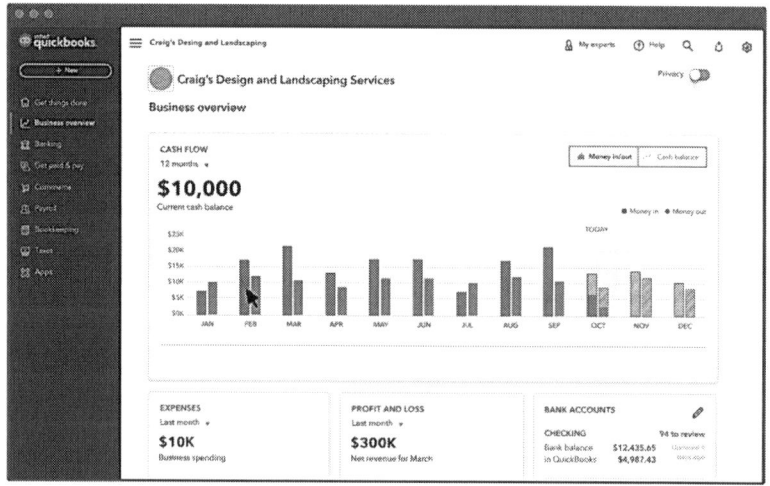

The QuickBooks Online Business View: A Smarter Way to Manage Your Data

QuickBooks Online provides up-to-date and relevant business statistics through its intuitive dashboard. Here's how to set it up and get started:

1. Setting Up the Dashboard

QuickBooks offers two display options: Business View and Accountant View.

- **Business View:** For business owners and managers, this view uses simple, non-accounting-specific terminology.
- **Accountant View**: For accountants, it provides specific terminology and tools relevant to their work.

To change your view, click the gear icon located in the top right of your screen.

Next, add users to your setup:

The main user should be assigned to the "primary admin" role.

Add more administrators and regular users while setting their privileges depending on the purpose of their work.

2. Entering Your Company Details

Fill in your company details:

1. Click the gear icon in the top-right corner.

2. Choose Account and Settings > Company.

3. Provide your business name, upload your logo, and add contact details, including the physical and legal addresses.

These provide the details that ensure your QuickBooks profile is complete, illustrating your business identity across reports and communications.

3. Sales Settings Setup

Sales and expense settings are two of the most important elements in generating reports. In setting this up:

1. Go to Account and Settings > Sales and Expenses tabs.

2. Make the following adjustments:

- **Sales Form Design:** Personalize your invoices with your logo and format.
- **Invoice Automation:** Enable features like automatic reminders for unpaid invoices.
- **VAT Settings**: Fill in the VAT details to handle tax compliance.
- Year-End Date: Specify the date on which the financial reports will be closed.

You can also turn on features like sales tracking by customer or the ability to create purchase orders, depending on your business.

By setting up QuickBooks Online to fit your specific needs, you'll find yourself working smarter-not harder. Whether you're a seasoned business owner or just starting out, QuickBooks is able to fit your needs.

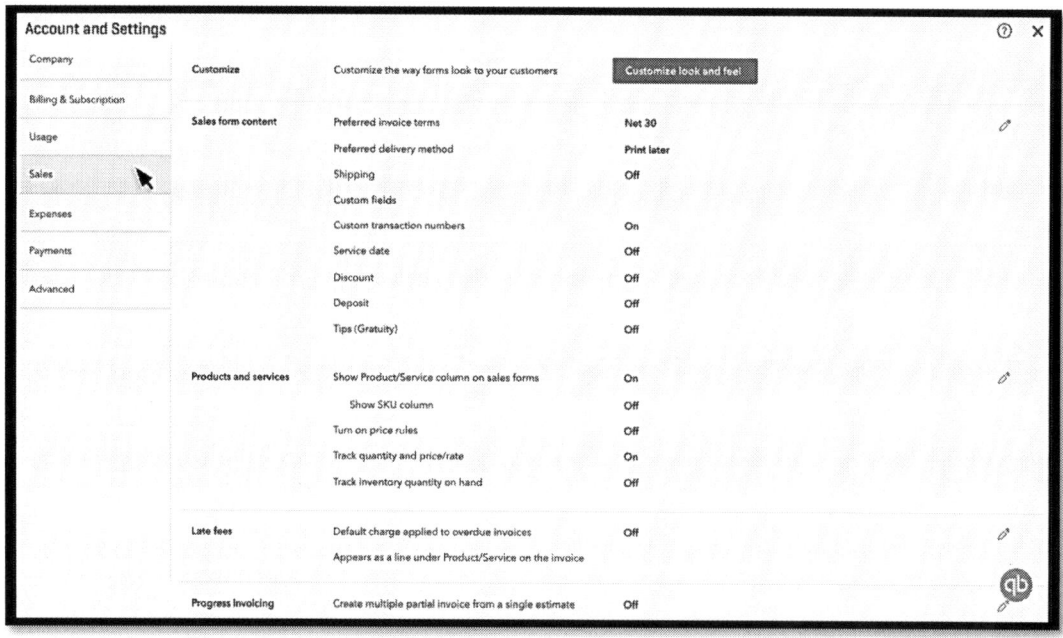

Adjusting your sales settings is just the beginning when it comes to generating accurate financial reports in QuickBooks Online. Follow these steps to import your data, link accounts, and integrate essential tools.

4. Import Your Business Data

Simplify your transition to QuickBooks by uploading existing business data:

- Click the gear icon for Settings, then select Import Data.
- Upload spreadsheets containing details about customers, suppliers, products, invoices, and more.

- QuickBooks supports popular file formats, including MS Excel and CSV, making the process seamless.

5. Link Your Bank Accounts

To streamline tracking of your transactions, connect your bank accounts and credit cards:

- Go to Settings > Account and Settings > Bill Pay > Bank Accounts.
- Once linked, your transactions will sync automatically, making reconciliation and expense tracking faster and more accurate.

6. Integrate Payroll Software

QuickBooks allows integration with various payroll providers, including its own QuickBooks Payroll:

- If using QuickBooks Payroll, you'll see a dedicated Payroll tab on your dashboard for easy navigation.
- This integration simplifies tax calculations, automates employee payments, and ensures compliance with payroll laws.

7. Add Other Integrations

Extend QuickBooks' functionality by connecting it to other software tools:

- Explore the QuickBooks App Store for integrations that suit your business needs, such as tools for sales, marketing, compliance, or cash flow forecasting.
- With hundreds of apps available, you can tailor your QuickBooks experience to match your operations seamlessly.

8. Get Ready for Tax Season

Stay ahead of your tax obligations by preparing early:

- Research and note key federal, state, and local tax due dates.
- If using QuickBooks Payroll, it offers built-in tax reporting features to help you stay compliant.
- Don't forget to input your federal and state tax ID numbers for accurate reporting.

By following these steps, you'll set up a powerful and customized financial management system with QuickBooks Online. From syncing data to preparing for tax season, QuickBooks ensures you stay organized and in control of your business finances.

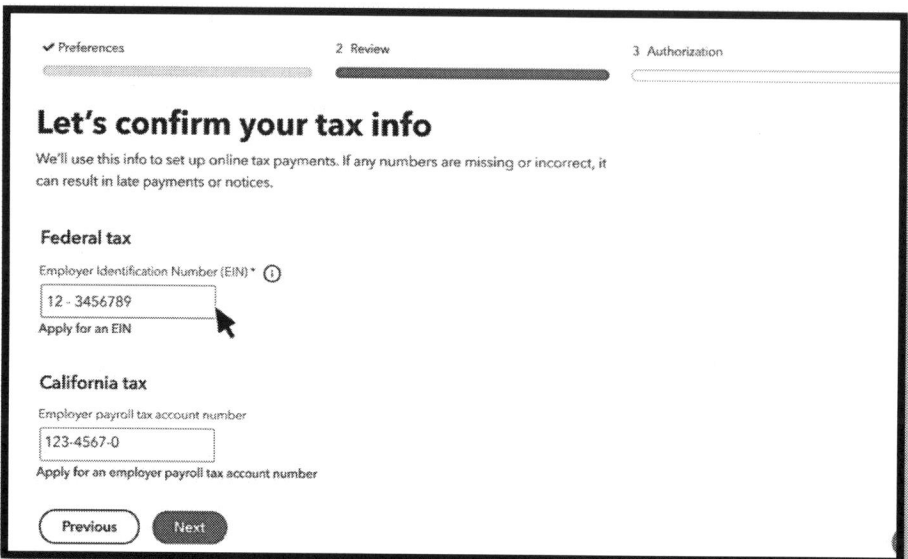

Simplify Tax Season with QuickBooks Payroll

Taking care of your QuickBooks Payroll tax details now will make tax season much smoother later on. Here's a guide on how to properly reconcile in QuickBooks Online:

How to Reconcile in QuickBooks Online

Reconciliation is the process of comparing your financial records with your supporting documents to identify and correct any discrepancies. Follow these steps to ensure your accounts are in order:

1. Review or Enter the Opening Balance

Start by checking your opening balance:

- Navigate to Settings and select the Reconcile tab under Tools.
- Verify that your starting balance is accurate or input it if necessary.

2. Address Discrepancies with the Opening Balance

If the opening balance doesn't match your records:

- Check the discrepancy report, which QuickBooks will guide you to.
- Make any necessary adjustments to correct the balance.

3. Check the Audit History

If discrepancies persist due to multiple changes:

- Click View under the History section to access the Audit History.
- This will help you track all changes made to transactions, so you can pinpoint what caused the discrepancy and correct it.

By following these steps, you'll have your QuickBooks accounts fully reconciled, ensuring that your financial records are accurate and ready for tax season.

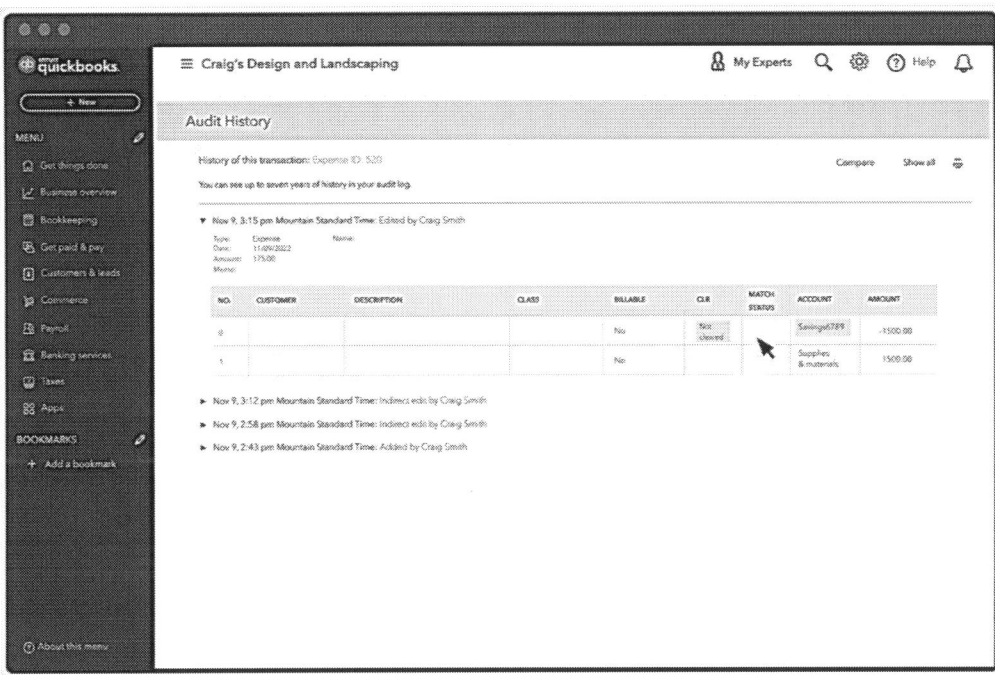

The "Audit History" section provides key details such as the customer, transaction amount, and any additional descriptions associated with the entry.

How to Undo Reconciliation in QuickBooks Online

If your reconciliation has too many discrepancies, it might be easier to reverse the reconciliation and start fresh. Here's how you can do it, either with the help of an accountant or manually:

Adding an Accountant to Undo Reconciliation

If you need an accountant to handle the reversal:

1. Go to Settings > Manage Users > Accounting Firms > Invite.

Once your accountant has access, they can:

- Go to the Reconcile page.
- Click the History by Account button in the top-right corner to reverse the reconciliation in bulk, without needing to edit each transaction individually.

Manually Undo Reconciliation

Alternatively, you can undo the reconciliation by manually adjusting each transaction:

1. Navigate to the Accounting menu and select Your Company > Chart of Accounts.

2. Choose the relevant account and click View Register.

3. Uncheck the R status and replace it with either a blank status or C for cleared.

4. Click Save, then confirm by selecting Yes.

By following these steps, you'll be able to either work with your accountant or manually undo a reconciliation and correct any discrepancies in your QuickBooks Online account.

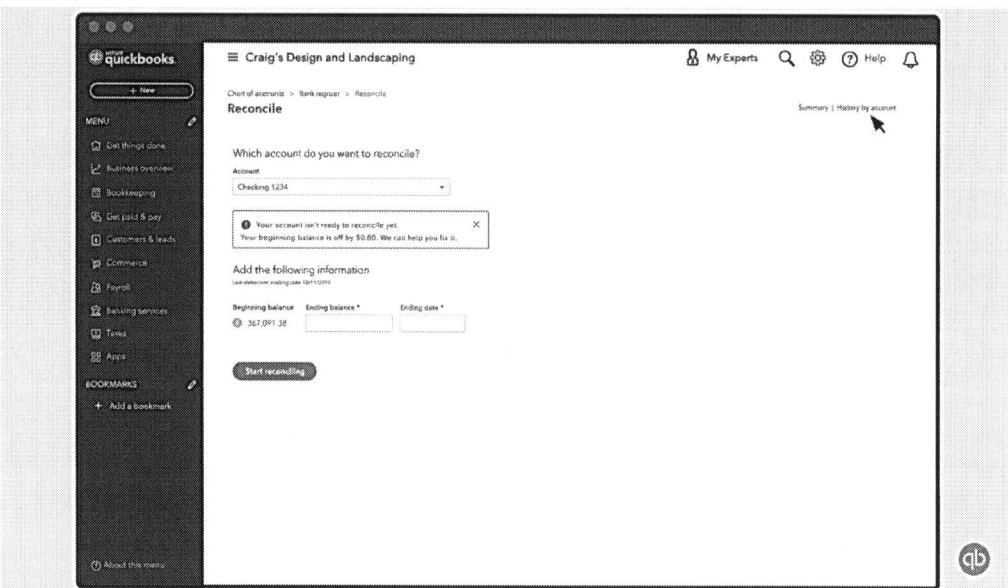

The "History by Account" button is on the top-right of the "Reconcile" page.

HOW TO DELETE A DEPOSIT IN QUICKBOOKS ONLINE

If you have to delete a deposit-either because it was entered by mistake or is a duplicate-follow these steps:

1. Go to Settings > Banking >Make Deposits.

2. If the "Payments to Deposit" box appears, click Cancel.

3. Click Previous to go through existing transactions and find the deposit to delete.

4. Select Edit> Delete Deposit.

HOW TO USE THE QUICKBOOKS MOBILE APP

Although QuickBooks Online is best accessed on a desktop, the mobile app is perfect for managing tasks while on the move, such as handling invoices, scanning receipts, and tracking expenses or mileage.

To get started, download the QuickBooks Accounting app from the App Store or the QuickBooks Online Accounting app from Google Play. After logging in, tap the "+" symbol located at the bottom center of the homepage to open the main menu and select the task you want to perform.

QuickBooks Online Alternatives

While QuickBooks Online is the top choice for accounting software thanks to its robust feature set, reporting tools, and reliable support, there are alternatives like FreshBooks that might suit specific needs, especially for ecommerce businesses. FreshBooks provides a similar set of features at a lower price, including inventory management on all plans—something QuickBooks reserves for its higher-tier options.

WHAT'S NEW IN QUICKBOOKS ONLINE 2025

System Requirements for QuickBooks Online Products

To ensure the best experience with QuickBooks Online products (including QuickBooks Online Accountant, Payroll, Self-Employed, Sole Trader, and QuickBooks Time), make sure your system and browser meet the necessary requirements.

Internet Speed and Browser Compatibility

QuickBooks Online products perform best depending on your internet speed, operating system, and browser. Keep in mind that QuickBooks Online offers different experiences on web and mobile devices.

For Linux users, QuickBooks Online and its related products are accessible via a web browser, but the QuickBooks Online Advanced desktop app is not supported.

SUPPORTED BROWSERS

QuickBooks Online supports the current version of browsers and the two prior versions. Older versions may not work as expected. The supported browsers include:

- **Google Chrome**: Version 78 or later
- **Mozilla Firefox**: Version 76 or later (Note: Mac users must install the Firefox PDF plugin to preview and print forms)
- **Microsoft Edge**: Version 79 or later
- **Safari:** Version 12 or later (Mac only)
- **Opera**: Version 68 or later
- **Samsung Internet:** Version 10 or later

Important Note: QuickBooks no longer supports Internet Explorer.

SYSTEM REQUIREMENTS - QUICKBOOKS ONLINE

To use QuickBooks Online effectively, your system must meet the following requirements:

For Computers:

- **PC:** A computer with at least a 1 GHz processor, 256 MB of RAM, and Windows 7 or later.
- **Mac:** An Intel-based Mac running macOS X 10.6 or newer.
- **Note:** QuickBooks Online does not support Linux operating systems, including Ubuntu and Fedora.

Internet and Display:

- **Internet:** A high-speed connection such as DSL, cable, or T1 is required.
- **Display:** A screen resolution of at least 1024x768 is recommended.

Printing:

- **For Windows users**: Adobe Reader version 7.0 or newer is necessary to print forms.
- **Printers:** A laser or inkjet printer is required. Dot-matrix printers are not supported.

Supported Browsers for Windows:

Make sure to check the specific system requirements for each browser on their developer's website:

- Google Chrome (with automatic updates).
- Mozilla Firefox (with automatic updates).
- Microsoft Internet Explorer: Version 10 or later (32-bit version recommended).

Supported Browsers for macOS:

Refer to the browser developer's site for specific system requirements:

- Apple Safari 6.1 or later.
- Google Chrome (with automatic updates).
- Mozilla Firefox (with automatic updates).
- Note: Firefox requires the PDF Plugin for printing and previewing forms.

FREQUENTLY ASKED QUESTIONS

- **Export to Excel**: QuickBooks Online works with Excel 97 or newer.
- **Accessing QuickBooks on Tablets or Mobile Devices**: Compatible with supported browsers on iOS, Android, and Windows 8 devices.
- **Exporting to QuickBooks or Quicken Desktop (U.S. only)**: Requires a supported version of Internet Explorer with an ActiveX component.

COMPATIBLE BROWSERS FOR TABLETS AND MOBILE DEVICES

iPhone / iPad:

- Requires iOS 7.1.1 or later.
- Use Safari with Private Mode turned off to enable the cookies necessary for QuickBooks Online.
- Third-party browsers like Chrome or Dolphin may work but are not officially supported.

Android Devices:

- Android version 4.2.2 (Jelly Bean) or newer.
- The Chrome browser is recommended for the best performance.

Surface / Windows 8 Devices:

- Internet Explorer 10 or newer in Desktop Mode is required.
- Note: Windows Phone 8 is not supported.

This version maintains the structure and content but simplifies the language for better readability.

GET STARTED WITH QUICKBOOKS IN JUST A FEW MINUTES

As a small business owner, you're juggling countless responsibilities—minimizing expenses, tracking finances, sending invoices, and organizing records to make tax season less stressful. Managing your financial health is crucial for the future of your business, but many entrepreneurs rely on scattered tools like spreadsheets, paper receipts, email invoices, and bank records. This approach can quickly spiral into chaos, making it tough to stay organized.

QuickBooks Online provides an easy-to-use, cloud-based solution designed to simplify how you handle your business finances. It integrates seamlessly into most small business workflows, making it an invaluable tool for managing your accounts.

That said, if you're just starting out, setting up QuickBooks Online might seem overwhelming. With so many menus, options, and features, it can be hard to figure out where to start or what to focus on first.

To make it easier, here's a straightforward, step-by-step guide to help you set up QuickBooks Online and get comfortable using it.

This version is more conversational and approachable while preserving the structure and context of the original content.

Your First 15 Minutes with QuickBooks Online

GETTING STARTED WITH QUICKBOOKS ONLINE

If you're new to QuickBooks Online, this guide is designed to help you dive into bookkeeping and start managing your finances right away. Our step-by-step articles will walk you through everything—from your very first sign-in to preparing for future financial quarters and beyond.

While we provide an estimated timeline for each task, it's important to move at your own pace. Taking the time to understand each step thoroughly will pay off in the long run. Just remember to follow the steps in the suggested order to ensure a smooth setup. If you're more interested in specific features or tasks, check out our "Setting up for Success with QuickBooks Online" series for targeted guidance.

Welcome to QuickBooks Online!

We're here to help you set up your business for accounting success from the very beginning. Before you can start sending invoices, though, there are a few key decisions to make about your accounts and preferences.

This version is conversational, user-friendly, and ensures the context and format remain intact.

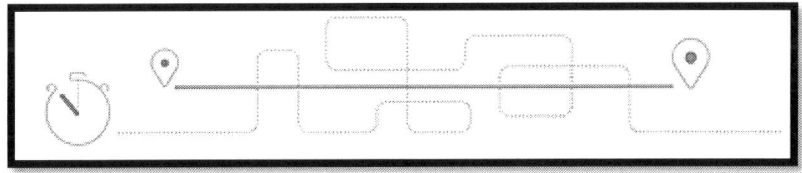

Minute 1: Align QuickBooks Online with Real-Life Transactions

According to our expert trainers, who bring years of experience in both product use and accounting, the golden rule for using QuickBooks Online is this: everything you record in QuickBooks should mirror what happens in real life.

This includes everything from recording transactions and sales to documenting bank deposits. While some actions, like sending invoices or accepting payments, are done directly within QuickBooks, many others—such as depositing funds into your bank— occur outside the system.

QuickBooks serves as your accounting tool, not the originator of every process. For instance, when you process credit card payments through your POS system, pay employees using QuickBooks Payroll, or take out a business loan, ensure your QuickBooks records match the real-world details. This includes names, dates, payment methods, and totals, which should align with your bank or credit card statements.

By keeping your QuickBooks entries consistent with actual events, you'll maintain accurate and hassle-free accounting!

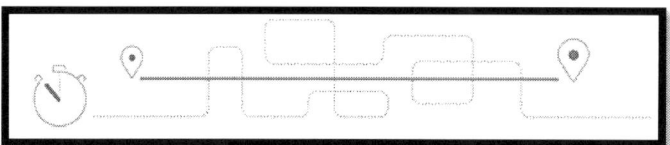

Minute 2: Set Up Your Company Information

Before you start entering any transactions in QuickBooks, it's important to fill in your company details. These details will automatically show up on your invoices and sales forms, so make sure everything is accurate.

To review or update your company information, follow these steps:

1. Click on the Gear Icon in QuickBooks.

2. Navigate to Account and Settings > Company.

3. Ensure the following details are complete and correct:

- Company Name
- Business Address (You can use a PO Box as the "Customer-Facing" address, but don't forget to include your legal address.)
- Email Address

- Website
- Phone Number

Getting these details right from the start ensures a professional and seamless experience for both you and your customers.

This version maintains the structure and context while simplifying the language for readability.

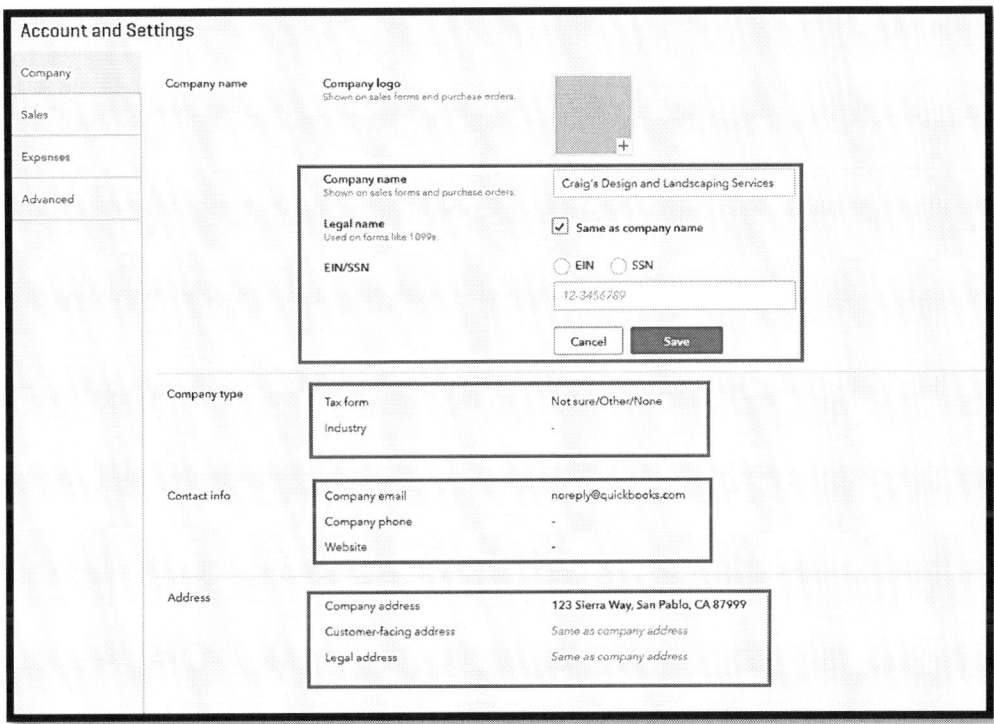

To edit any of this information, simply click the Pencil Icon in the corner, make your changes, and click "Save" when you're finished.

Next, make sure the correct company type and tax form you intend to file at the end of the fiscal year are selected.

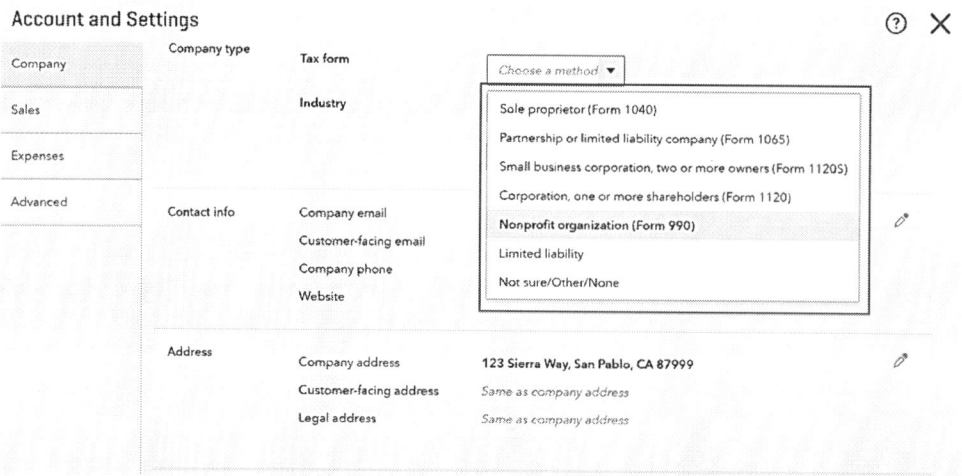

You'll also need to provide your EIN (Employer Identification Number) or Social Security Number, as required by law. If you're unsure which one applies to your business, it's best to consult your accountant or reach out to the IRS for advice.

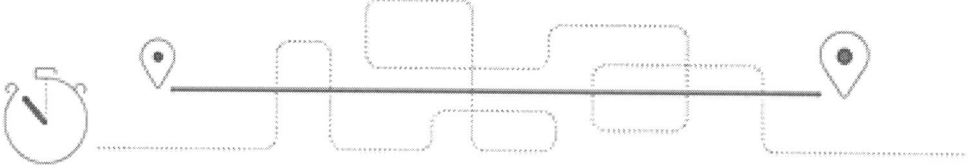

Minute 4: Set Your Fiscal Year Start Date

To set the start and end dates of the fiscal year for your business go **to Settings > Account and Settings > Accounting.** For most businesses, the fiscal year starts in January since it coincides with the income tax year. As a business owner, you should know your tax year schedule.

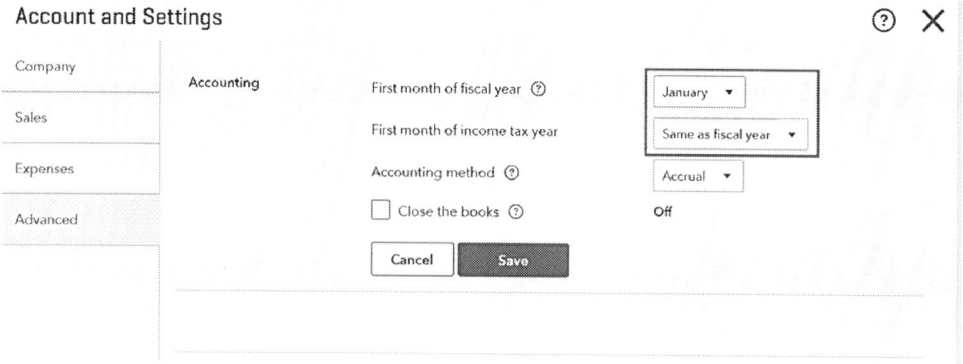

While you're at it, consider setting a "closing date" for your books, ideally 12 months from your start date. This feature helps protect your QuickBooks data from unauthorized changes as you prepare for tax filing. If you prefer, you can always set it up later.

Minute 5: Choose Your Accounting Method: Cash or Accrual

Go to Settings > Account and Settings > Accounting to decide whether your business will use the cash or accrual method for reporting income. Many new businesses opt for cash-basis bookkeeping because it's simpler—you only record income and expenses when they're actually received or paid. However, both methods have their own benefits, so it's worth considering what works best for your business.

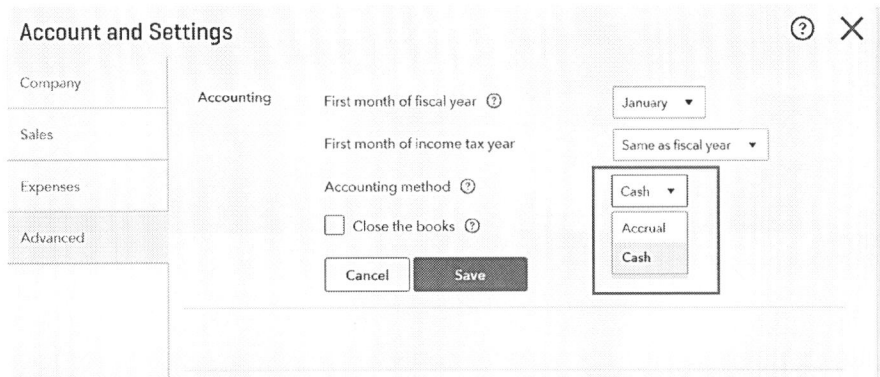

For more details about cash and accrual methods, check out our article in the QuickBooks Encyclopedia. It's important to pick the right accounting method upfront, as switching later can be tricky (though not impossible). If you're unsure which option is best, consult with your accountant or even a fellow business owner for guidance.

Minute 6: Set Your Accounting Currency

How are you holding up so far? If you need a quick break or have questions, feel free to drop them in the comments section below.

Now, head over to **Settings > Account and Settings > Advanced > Currency** to choose your home currency. This will be the currency you use to accept customer payments. If your business handles transactions in foreign currencies, enable the multicurrency feature to track them accurately.

This version keeps the format intact, simplifies the language, and maintains the context while making it more conversational and approachable.

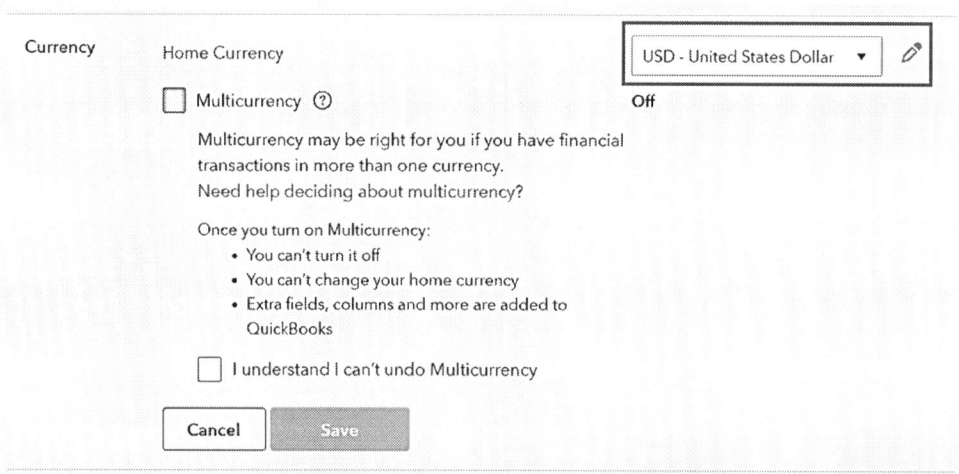

Be cautious: Once the multicurrency feature is enabled, you won't be able to change your home currency. If you need to make adjustments afterward, your only options are to either delete all your company data and start fresh or cancel your subscription and create a new account.

Minute 7: Upload Your Company Logo

With the basic setup complete, it's time to add a personal touch to your QuickBooks account.

Your logo is a critical part of your brand, appearing on the invoices, estimates, and sales receipts you send to customers. To make the best impression, follow these quick tips:

- **Shape:** Square or circular logos (that fit within a square) work best. Rectangular logos may stretch.
- **Background:** Use a white background for seamless integration with your forms.
- **File Formats**: Acceptable formats include .gif, .bmp, .png, .jpg, .jpe, or .jpeg.
- **Size**: The file must be smaller than 1MB.
- **Color Settings**: Use the RGB color space with a bit depth of 24-bits or lower.

We'll explore more invoice customization options later, but if you're ready to dive in now, check out our guide on customizing invoices in QuickBooks Online.

Minute 8: Set Default Invoice Payment Terms

Now, let's get you ready to send your first invoice! Go to Settings > Sales > Sales Form Content to choose your default payment terms.

- If you want customers to pay right away, select "Due on Receipt."
- For more flexibility, pick a timeframe from the dropdown menu.
- To offer custom payment terms or early payment discounts, click "+ Add New" to create them.

This version maintains the original structure and context, while using conversational and user-friendly language for clarity and engagement.

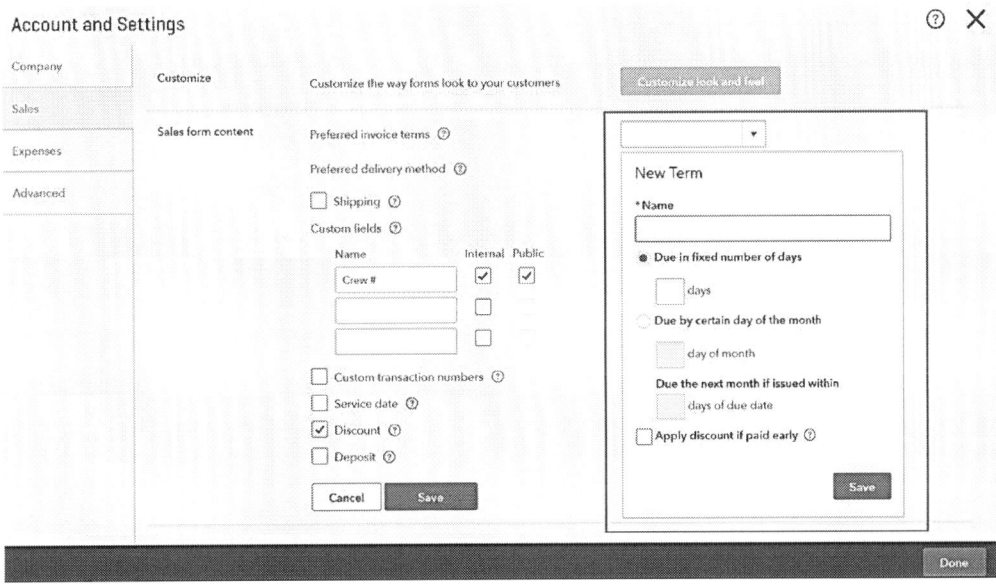

The default payment terms will automatically apply to most of your invoices, but you can always customize them for individual invoices directly on the form. Take some time to explore the settings, but don't worry—we'll revisit this menu later.

Minute 9: Set Up Sales Tax

If your business involves selling products, collecting sales tax is required in most states. Before starting this step, ensure your accounting method has already been selected.

When you access the Tax tab for the first time, QuickBooks will guide you through the setup process. You'll be prompted to specify where your products are sold to determine the appropriate sales tax rates.

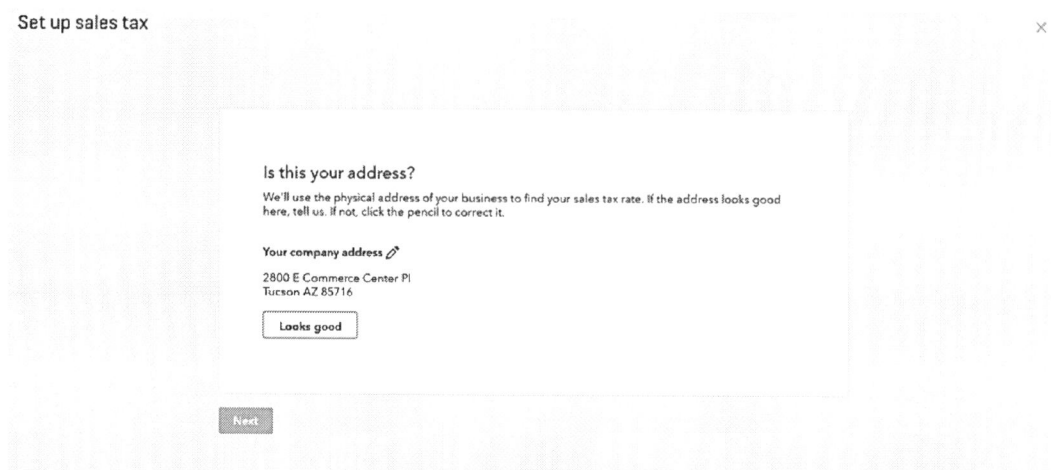

Set up sales tax

Is this your address?

We'll use the physical address of your business to find your sales tax rate. If the address looks good here, tell us. If not, click the pencil to correct it.

Your company address ✎

2800 E Commerce Center Pl
Tucson AZ 85716

Looks good

Next

This step is crucial because QuickBooks Online's Automated Sales Tax Center calculates sales tax using the accrual method, regardless of your selected accounting method. Here's how it works:

If you set your accounting method to Cash before configuring the Sales Tax Center, you'll default to manual sales tax calculations. [Learn more here.]

If you switch to the Cash method after setting up the Sales Tax Center, QuickBooks will still calculate sales tax automatically, but the data in your Sales Tax Center will reflect the accrual method. To reconcile this, you can review Sales Tax Liability reports to ensure your sales tax payments are recorded correctly in QuickBooks Online.

Finally, decide whether you want QuickBooks to handle your sales tax calculations automatically. Once you specify your tax period start date and filing frequency, this setting will be permanently enabled.

If you prefer to manage your sales tax manually, that's perfectly fine too—just follow the steps outlined above.

Minute 12: QuickBooks Test Drive - Practice Creating an Invoice

Before diving in with your real data, it's a great idea to get some hands-on practice. We highly recommend using the QuickBooks Test Drive feature to explore the invoicing tools. During your first few weeks with QuickBooks Online, Test Drive allows you to experiment with practice data instead of live transactions. Keep in mind that Test Drive mimics the functionality of QuickBooks Online Plus.

Once in Test Drive, click the Global Create Button (also called the Action Icon). This is your starting point for most transactions in QuickBooks. (For more information, check out our "Setting Up for Success with QuickBooks Online – The Fundamentals" guide.)

Take your time exploring each section of the invoice form and familiarize yourself with the type of information required in each field. Over the next hour, we'll work together to build these databases step-by-step.

This version retains the original structure, simplifies the language for clarity, and maintains a professional yet approachable tone.

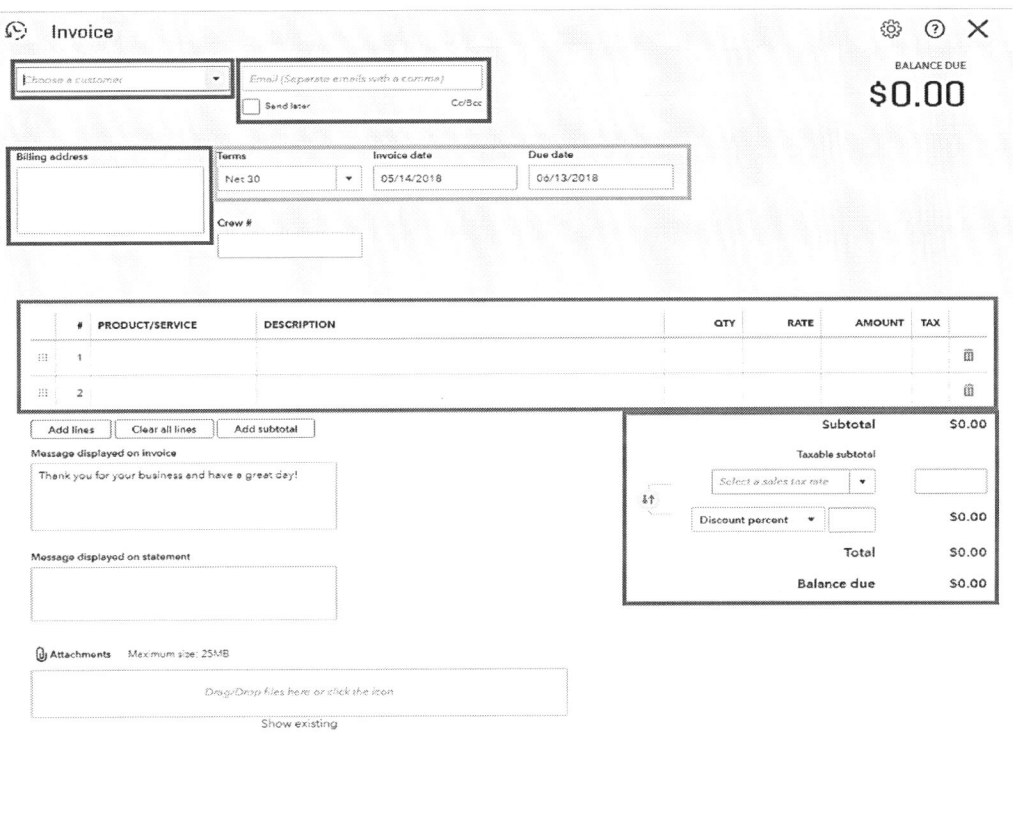

Why Test Drive is Valuable

The Test Drive feature provides you with sample data to experiment with, giving you a chance to explore how QuickBooks functions without affecting your actual business data. It's a risk-free way to familiarize yourself with the system.

In Test Drive, you'll practice creating an invoice using pre-loaded customer, account, and product information. This helps you immediately identify any gaps, offering clarity on what you'll need to focus on as you move forward with setting up your own products, services, and customers.

This version retains the original format and meaning while rephrasing for clarity and readability.

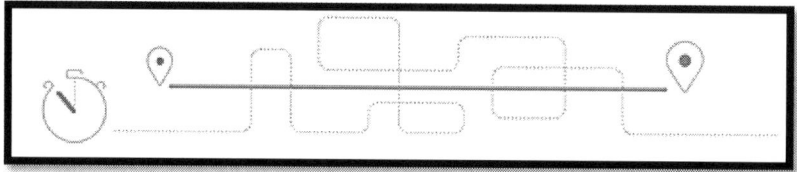

Finished!

Take a Moment to Reflect on Your Goals

Now that you've covered the basics, it's time to think about what you want to accomplish with your bookkeeping.

At the very least, you'll need to track all sales and expenses to gain a clear understanding of your business's financial health. Features like Online Banking and Payroll can streamline your accounting process and help keep everything organized.

How much you decide to use QuickBooks Online depends entirely on your business needs. You might choose to:

- Record daily sales and immediate income only.
- Focus solely on larger asset and liability accounts (keeping in mind that you'll need to account for anything you exclude).
- Enter all your financial data but selectively automate updates for specific online accounts.

Your decision will depend on your business's financial priorities—tracking what matters most to make informed decisions. Take a few minutes to write down your accounting goals. Having clear goals will help you determine which features in QuickBooks Online deserve your attention.

NAVIGATING THE INTERFACE LIKE A PRO

Get Familiar with the QuickBooks Online Navigation Menu

QuickBooks Online makes managing your finances easier with its customizable navigation menu. You can personalize it to fit your workflow, putting your most-used pages just a click away and saving valuable time.

The best way to explore this feature is by following along directly in QuickBooks Online.

Navigation Menu Overview

The improved navigation menu is designed for both business owners and accountants, offering a seamless experience. It includes a single menu that serves both business and accountant views, and you can toggle between the two as needed.

You can also customize your view by expanding or collapsing different sections of the menu to suit your preferences and make navigation more convenient.

This version maintains the original structure and intent while simplifying the language to make it more relatable and user-friendly.

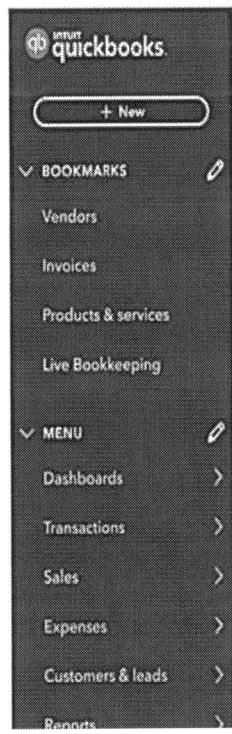 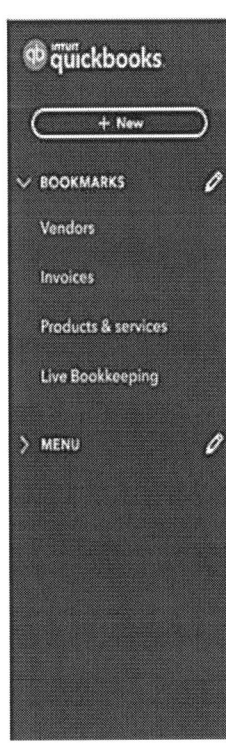 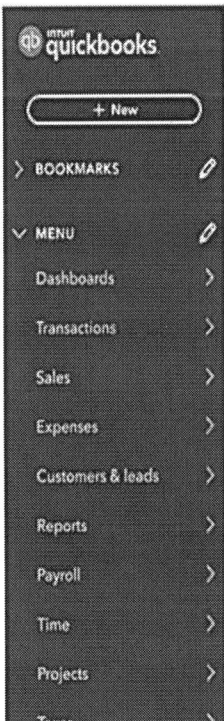 

Understanding Your QuickBooks Online Navigation Menu

Here's an overview of the QuickBooks Online navigation menu and how each option helps you manage your business efficiently:

- **Bookmarks:** Quickly access your most frequently used pages.
- **Hover and Flyout**: Hover over a main menu item to see its sub-menu options.
- **Dashboards**: Create, plan, budget, and manage your finances from one place. Includes a customizable home page, cash flow insights, and a financial planner.
- **Transactions:** Import, categorize, and review bank or app transactions. Manage receipts, reconcile accounts, and oversee your chart of accounts.
- **Sales**: Access the invoicing center and track your income trends over time.
- **Expenses:** Monitor expense activities, including vendor payments and mileage tracking.
- **Customers & Leads**: Manage customer information, track leads, and market to customers using integrations like Mailchimp.
- **Reports:** Analyze company data, track progress, organize key activities, and make informed decisions.
- **Payroll:** Oversee employee and contractor management, including time tracking, benefits, and tax compliance.
- **Time:** Use QuickBooks Time to manage employee schedules and tasks, integrating seamlessly with payroll and invoicing.
- **Projects (Plus and Advanced):** Track the profitability of specific projects, along with related income and expenses, supported by project-specific reports.
- **Taxes:** Automate tax setup and ensure compliance, including filing 1099 forms for contractors.
- **Lending & Banking:** Access tools like QuickBooks Checking, business funding, and commerce options for tracking sales.
- **My Accountant**: Collaborate directly with your accountant within QuickBooks.
- **Apps**: Discover additional QuickBooks tools and third-party integrations to enhance functionality.

- **Live Experts:** For businesses without an accountant, a dedicated bookkeeping team is available to help manage your books or assist with setup.

Customizing Your Navigation Menu

Tailor the navigation menu to suit your workflow:

- Choose your preferred layout.
- Add shortcuts for pages you frequently visit.
- Hide sections you don't need to keep things streamlined.

This version maintains the original content while presenting it in a simpler, more conversational tone.

Bookmarking Pages in QuickBooks Online

To bookmark a page:

1. Click Edit next to the BOOKMARKS dropdown.

2. Select the pages you want to appear in the BOOKMARKS column.

3. To reorder them, click Reorder and drag the pages into your preferred sequence.

4. Click Save when you're done.

Tip: You can also bookmark a page by selecting Bookmark this page in the BOOKMARKS column. This is especially useful for pages not listed in the main or sub-menus.

To remove a bookmark:

1. Click Edit next to the BOOKMARKS dropdown.

2. Uncheck the pages you want to remove.

3. Click Save to confirm.

To hide or show a page:

1. Click Edit next to the MENU dropdown.

2. Check the pages you want to display or uncheck the ones to hide.

3. To rearrange them, select Reorder and drag them as needed.

4. Click Save to finalize your changes.

CHOOSING THE BEST QUICKBOOKS PLAN FOR YOUR BUSINESS

In today's fast-paced business world, efficient financial management is crucial for small and medium-sized businesses. Whether you're working to close deals, secure funding, or increase profits, having the right tools to manage your finances can make all the difference. This is where QuickBooks Online shines as a valuable asset for small businesses.

At Rigits Bookkeeping & Accounting, we understand the daily challenges business owners face. That's why we're committed to providing the financial support and tools needed to make managing your finances simple and effective. QuickBooks Online isn't just about tracking numbers—it's about empowering business owners to make informed decisions, maintain financial health, and free up time to focus on growing their business.

This guide is designed to make learning QuickBooks Online straightforward and stress-free. Whether you're a new user or want to unlock more features, you'll see that mastering this platform is achievable with the right approach. Let's explore how QuickBooks Online can simplify your financial tasks while aligning with Rigits' mission to help clients reach significant milestones confidently.

Additional Resources

As part of this guide, we've included links to related tutorials on our site, such as:

- How to calculate retained earnings
- The differences between cash and accrual accounting
- Gross profit versus net profit

By the end of this tutorial, you'll have the tools and knowledge to streamline your financial management with ease.

Key Takeaways:

- QuickBooks Online provides an efficient and user-friendly solution for managing small to medium-sized businesses.
- You can enhance QuickBooks Online's core functionality with third-party integrations to streamline your business operations.

- The platform offers valuable insights that help improve cash flow, drive growth, and boost overall success.

WHY QUICKBOOKS ONLINE?

QuickBooks Online is designed to simplify financial management for your business. Its intuitive dashboard provides an overview of key financial metrics, including cash flow, expenses, invoicing, and payroll, all in one place. With real-time updates, you'll always have access to the most accurate and up-to-date financial information, making it easier to manage and report your business finances.

One of QuickBooks Online's standout features is its integration capabilities. It seamlessly connects with third-party apps, such as e-commerce platforms, payment processors, and customer relationship management tools. This streamlines workflows, reduces errors, and offers a comprehensive view of your business's financial health within a single system.

Security first: QuickBooks Online uses advanced encryption and robust data protection measures to keep your financial information secure and accessible only to authorized users.

QuickBooks Online is tailored to meet the needs of businesses looking for efficient financial management tools. Whether you need to manage accounts payable/receivable, create detailed financial reports, or track expenses, it's all here. Plus, the mobile app allows you to manage your finances on the go.

At Rights Bookkeeping & Accounting, we recommend QuickBooks Online as the top choice for small business owners. It not only promotes growth but also provides clarity and frees up your time so you can focus on what matters most—running your business.

SETTING UP QUICKBOOKS ONLINE FOR FINANCIAL SUCCESS

Follow these steps to set up QuickBooks Online and take control of your business finances:

Step 1: Sign Up and Choose the Right Plan

QuickBooks Online offers four subscription options: Simple Start, Essentials, Plus, and Advanced. Each plan caters to different business needs, such as inventory tracking, time tracking, or multi-user access. Start with a free trial to explore the features before committing.

Step 2: Customize Your Settings

Once you're signed up, personalize QuickBooks to suit your business. Go to the Account and Settings menu to update your business details, tax preferences, and invoice appearance.

Step 3: Link Your Bank and Credit Card Accounts

Connect your bank and credit card accounts to QuickBooks to automate transaction imports. This not only saves time but also minimizes errors, giving you a real-time view of your cash flow for easier budgeting and forecasting.

Step 4: Organize Your Chart of Accounts

QuickBooks provides a default chart of accounts, but customizing it to match your business's operations improves financial reporting. Properly categorized transactions ensure accurate tracking of revenue, expenses, and other financial activities.

Step 5: Enter Opening Balances

If you're transitioning from another accounting system, it's important to input opening balances. Include bank balances, outstanding receivables, and initial asset or liability figures to maintain continuity in your records.

Step 6: Invite Your Accountant

Add your accountant to your QuickBooks account for professional financial management. This ensures accurate bookkeeping, simplifies tax filings, and allows for strategic financial planning to keep your business on track.

By following these steps, you'll unlock the full potential of QuickBooks Online, gaining critical insights into your business while saving valuable time. It's not just about managing your finances—it's about empowering your business to thrive.

CUSTOMIZING YOUR QUICKBOOKS ONLINE EXPERIENCE

Tailoring QuickBooks Online to suit your business needs can significantly improve how you manage your finances. Here's how to make the most of its features:

Make Your Dashboard Work for You

Your dashboard serves as the central hub of QuickBooks Online. Personalize it to display the most relevant information for your business, such as cash flow, sales, or expenses. By doing this, you'll have quick access to essential data, enabling faster, more informed decision-making.

Create Custom Reports

QuickBooks Online lets you build custom reports tailored to your business metrics. Whether it's a profit and loss statement or an expense breakdown, these reports provide insights specific to your operational needs, helping you track performance and plan effectively.

Integrate Third-Party Apps

Expand QuickBooks Online's capabilities by integrating third-party apps. These integrations can automate payroll, manage inventory, or handle customer relationships. By streamlining these processes, you save time, improve accuracy, and make your workflows more efficient.

Customizing QuickBooks Online ensures that your financial management system aligns with your business goals, paving the way for streamlined operations and growth.

AUTOMATING FOR EFFICIENCY

QuickBooks Online offers powerful automation features that simplify routine tasks, allowing you to focus on strategic growth.

- **Automate Routine Tasks**: Set up rules to automatically categorize transactions, send invoices, or pay bills. This ensures everything happens on time, without the risk of forgetting.
- **Reduce Errors**: Automation minimizes human error, making your processes more efficient and reliable.

- **Save Time:** By automating repetitive tasks, you free up time for other essential aspects of your business.

QuickBooks Online isn't just about managing your finances today—it's about building a system that evolves with your business, fostering long-term efficiency and growth.

MAXIMIZING REPORTING AND ANALYTICS

QuickBooks Online isn't only a bookkeeping tool—it's a comprehensive platform for generating insights that drive smart decision-making. Here's how you can leverage its reporting features:

Customizable Reports

QuickBooks Online allows you to create tailored reports focusing on metrics that matter most to your business. Whether it's tracking cash flow, monitoring expenses, or analyzing sales trends, you can adjust date ranges, financial metrics, and comparison periods to turn raw data into actionable insights.

Track Financial Performance in Real Time

Access up-to-date financial information with QuickBooks Online's real-time tracking of income statements, balance sheets, and cash flow. Having a clear view of your financial health helps you make timely decisions, address issues early, and seize opportunities as they arise.

Analyze Spending and Expenses

QuickBooks simplifies expense management by categorizing and comparing expenses over time. This allows you to identify potential savings, optimize spending, and improve profitability. Effective expense management is key to budgeting and financial planning, ensuring sustained business growth.

With these tools, QuickBooks Online empowers small businesses to transform financial data into a competitive edge. Paired with the expert guidance of Rigits Bookkeeping & Accounting, you'll be well-equipped to improve profitability, boost efficiency, and achieve lasting success.

SALES TREND ANALYSIS

For businesses focused on growth, understanding sales trends is vital. QuickBooks Online provides powerful tools to examine sales patterns, uncover seasonal trends, and identify your top-performing products or services. These insights enable you to optimize inventory management, fine-tune marketing efforts, and allocate resources more effectively.

FORECASTING AND BUDGETING

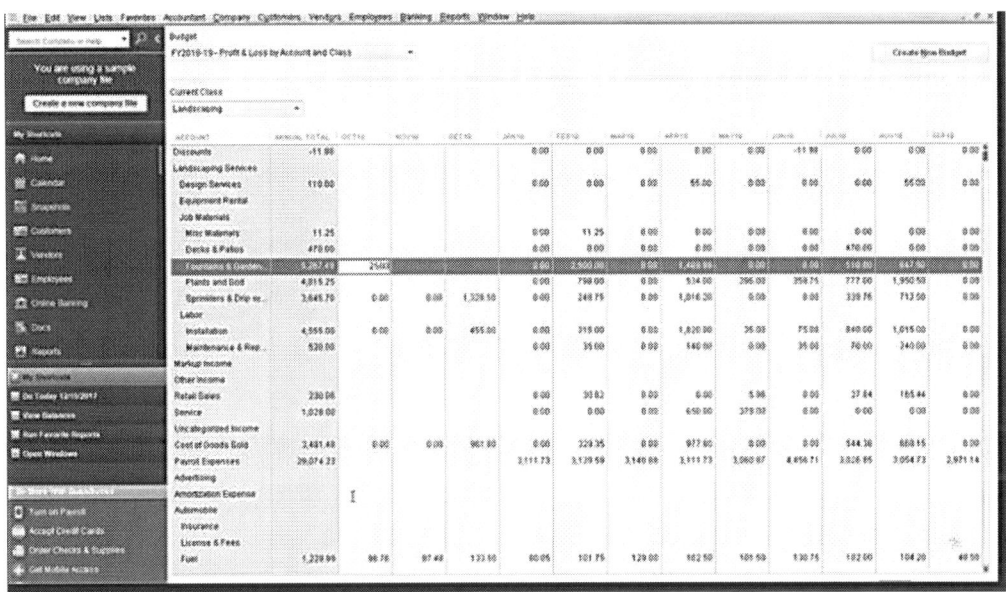

QuickBooks Online's analytics tools help businesses predict financial trends and create accurate budgets. By leveraging its forecasting capabilities, you can anticipate cash flow challenges, plan for major expenses, and set achievable financial goals. Effective forecasting and budgeting are essential for navigating unpredictable markets and ensuring long-term sustainability.

PARTNERING WITH RIGITS FOR SUCCESS

With Rigits Bookkeeping & Accounting as your trusted partner, you can maximize the potential of QuickBooks Online's reporting and analytics tools. Our expertise ensures that your QuickBooks is set up correctly and that you can interpret financial data with confidence. We're here to help you achieve your financial milestones and provide peace of mind, ensuring you always know where your business stands.

CHAPTER 2
MASTERING FINANCIAL BASICS

Streamline Your Finances with QuickBooks Online 2025

In today's fast-paced business world, effectively managing your finances is more crucial than ever. QuickBooks Online 2025 offers a robust solution for businesses of all sizes, simplifying accounting tasks, streamlining operations, and boosting productivity. Whether you're new to QuickBooks or an experienced user, mastering its features can revolutionize your financial management. This guide provides actionable tips and strategies to help you maximize the potential of QuickBooks Enterprise 2025 and set your business on the path to success.

WHAT IS QUICKBOOKS ENTERPRISE 2025?

Before diving into optimization strategies, it's essential to understand the features of QuickBooks Online 2025. Tailored for larger businesses with complex financial needs, this version offers:

- **Advanced Reporting**: Create detailed, customizable reports to analyze business performance.
  - **Inventory Management:** Monitor stock levels, streamline item tracking, and automate reordering.

- **User Permissions**: Assign role-specific access to ensure data security and control.
- **Seamless Integrations**: Connect with third-party applications to enhance workflows and efficiency.

By familiarizing yourself with these features, you'll be better equipped to leverage the software effectively.

GETTING STARTED: KEY SETUP TIPS

1. Define Your Business Structure

Identify whether your business operates as a sole proprietorship, partnership, or corporation. This foundational step ensures that your chart of accounts and financial reports align with your specific business needs.

2. Use the Setup Wizard

Take advantage of the Setup Wizard in QuickBooks Online 2025 to establish your company file. It guides you through essential steps like entering your business name, address, and fiscal year to ensure everything is configured correctly.

3. Customize Your Chart of Accounts

Personalize your chart of accounts to match your business operations. Organize it with clear categories for income, expenses, assets, and liabilities to create meaningful financial reports.

SIMPLIFYING OPERATIONS WITH QUICKBOOKS ONLINE 2025

1. Automate Recurring Transactions

Save time by automating recurring invoices, bills, and payroll. QuickBooks ensures transactions are processed on time, reducing manual effort and avoiding delays.

2. Leverage Advanced Reporting

Use advanced reporting tools to track key metrics like sales trends, department-wise expenses, and overall profitability. These insights empower you to make well-informed business decisions.

3. Monitor Real-Time Cash Flow

Stay on top of your finances with real-time cash flow monitoring. Regularly review reports to make smarter spending and investment choices.

ENHANCING INVENTORY MANAGEMENT

1. Track Inventory Levels

Utilize tools like barcode scanning and batch tracking to monitor inventory accurately within QuickBooks.

2. Set Reorder Points

Prevent stockouts by setting reorder thresholds for each item. QuickBooks will alert you when it's time to restock, ensuring smooth operations.

3. Conduct Regular Audits

Schedule periodic inventory checks to ensure your records in QuickBooks align with physical inventory, maintaining accurate financial data.

COLLABORATION AND USER MANAGEMENT

1. Enable Multi-User Mode

Assign specific roles and permissions to your team members to control data access, enhance security, and streamline workflows.

2. Foster Team Collaboration

Integrate communication tools like Slack or Microsoft Teams with QuickBooks to encourage collaboration, improve decision-making, and enhance task coordination.

MAXIMIZING TRAINING AND RESOURCES

1. Invest in Ongoing Training

Encourage your team to participate in online courses and webinars to stay updated on QuickBooks' latest features and tools.

2. Engage with the QuickBooks Community

Join the QuickBooks community to access expert advice, share insights, and stay informed on best practices through forums and user group meetings.

By following these steps and tips, you can transform QuickBooks Online 2025 into a powerful tool for efficient financial management. With advanced features and seamless integrations, you'll be equipped to drive growth, improve decision-making, and achieve long-term business success.

TROUBLESHOOTING AND MAINTENANCE

1. Keep Your Software Updated

Regularly update QuickBooks Online to maintain peak performance. Frequent updates ensure you have access to the latest features, security patches, and enhancements. Visit the QuickBooks website periodically to check for updates.

2. Leverage QuickBooks Support

If you encounter any issues, take advantage of QuickBooks' extensive support resources. Utilize online tutorials, help articles, and the dedicated support team to quickly resolve problems and keep your operations running smoothly.

Your Road to Mastery

Mastering QuickBooks Online 2025 is an ongoing journey. By applying these tips, you can streamline your financial processes, improve collaboration, and enhance overall business performance. Keep exploring and learning to fully unlock the potential of QuickBooks for sustained growth and success.

Core Features: Invoices, Expenses, and Sales

Boost your business's efficiency with QuickBooks Online Advanced. It provides:

- **Comprehensive Insights**: Gain detailed understanding of your finances through robust analytics.
- **Tailored Workflows**: Personalize workflows to suit your business operations.
- **Seamless Collaboration:** Enhance teamwork and coordination across your organization.

These features help drive business success, making QuickBooks a vital tool for long-term financial management.

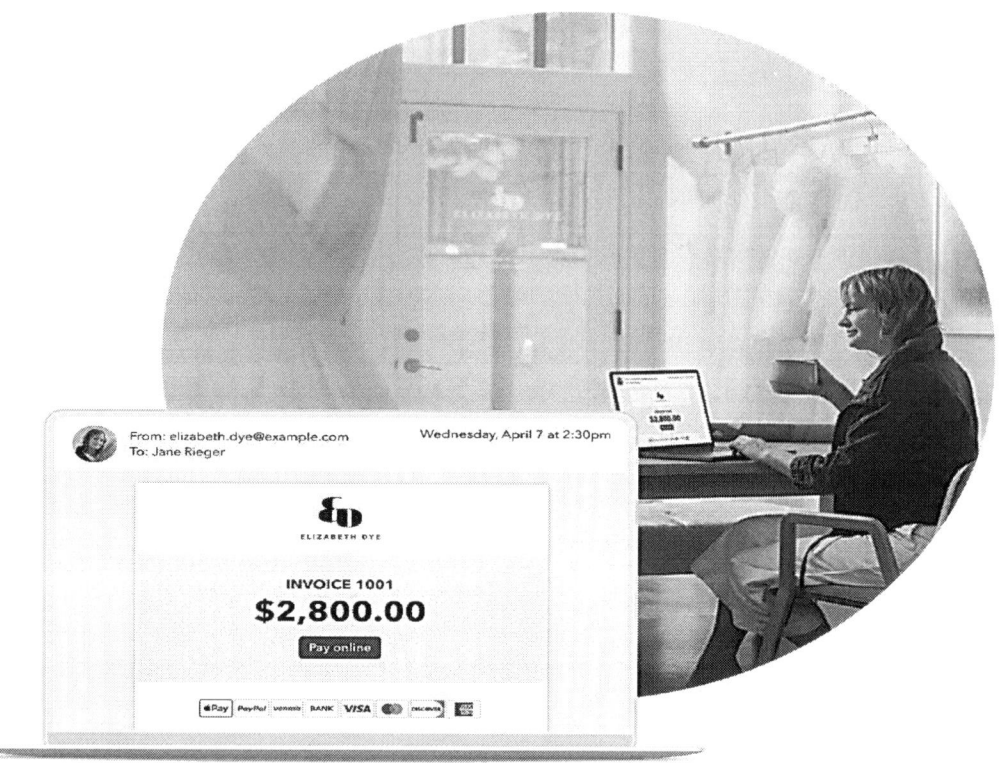

STREAMLINE YOUR INVOICING

- Stop tedious one-by-one invoice entry with batch invoicing.
- Create invoices 37% faster[1]
- Send or import several invoices in just a few clicks
- Duplicate similar invoices for different customers
- Available worldwide, except for broadcast use. You may choose to feature the business name or social handle

SIMPLIFY EXPENSE MANAGEMENT

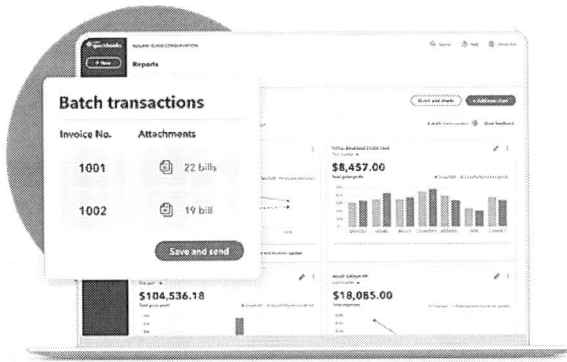

- **Save Time with Batch Expensing**: Streamline your workflow and free up time to focus on growing your business.
- **Effortless Expense Management**: Enter and update multiple expenses in just a few clicks.
- **Centralized Check Handling:** View and manage all your checks from a single screen.
- **Seamless Excel Integration:** Quickly copy and paste data from Excel into the batch transactions sheet for added convenience.

AUTOMATE YOUR INVOICING

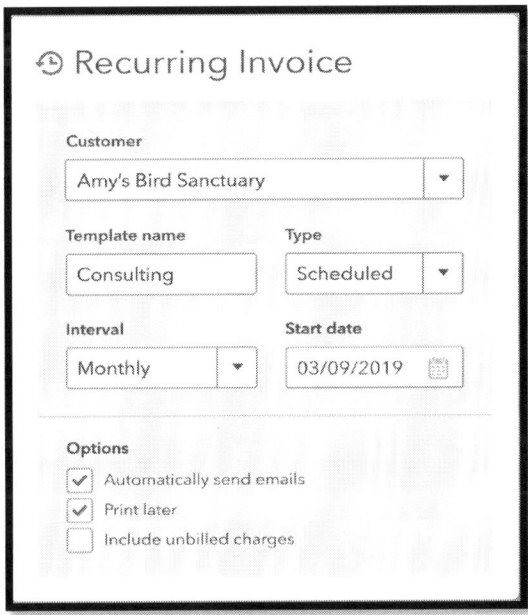

Effortless Invoicing with QuickBooks: QuickBooks' invoicing software makes managing invoices quick and accurate, giving you more time to focus on what you do best.

Set Up Recurring Invoices: Easily schedule recurring invoices and let QuickBooks take care of the rest. For added convenience, you can even send them out in batches.

Automated Payment Tracking: Forget about chasing payments! QuickBooks automatically tracks due and overdue invoices, sending personalized email reminders to late-paying clients, so you don't have to worry about follow-ups.

Streamlined Progress Invoicing: Manage large projects seamlessly with progress invoicing. Convert estimates into multiple invoices based on milestones or percentages of work completed. Send invoices in stages and accept online payments anytime, from any device.

TRACK INVOICE STATUS

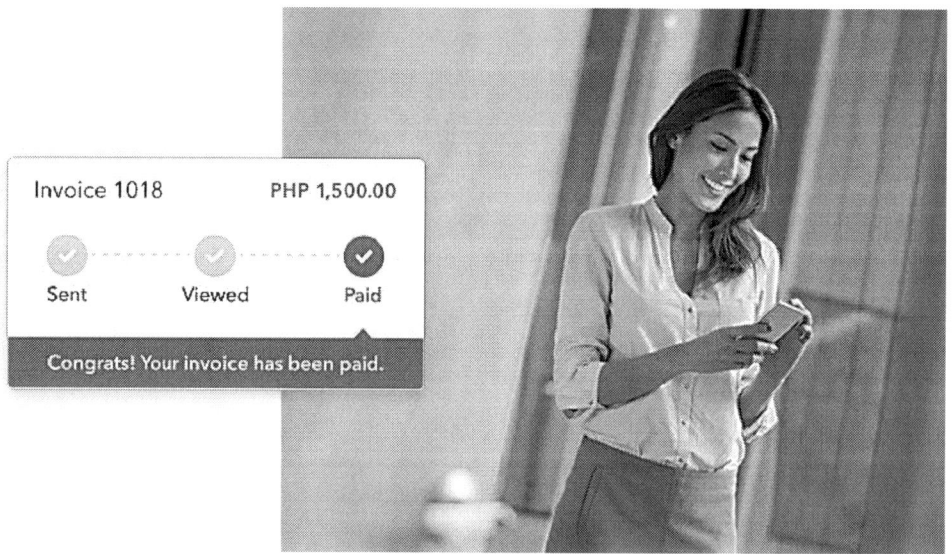

Track Invoice Status Effortlessly: Keep tabs on your payments with ease. QuickBooks instantly shows whether an invoice is paid or pending and automatically sends reminders to clients for overdue payments.

Automatic Calculations: QuickBooks simplifies your invoicing by automatically calculating VAT, discounts, and shipping costs, so you don't have to worry about the math.

Seamless International Invoicing: Reach clients worldwide with ease. QuickBooks lets you create and send invoices in multiple languages, including English, French, Spanish, Italian, Traditional Chinese, and Portuguese.

SUPPORTS MULTIPLE CURRENCIES

Exchange rate

$ Australian Dollars $1700.00

$ US Dollars $1100.00

QuickBooks supports more than 145 currencies. You can easily set exchange rates and invoice your clients anywhere around the world without hassle.

SETTING UP YOUR BUSINESS CHART OF ACCOUNTS

Getting started with QuickBooks Online means becoming familiar with the Chart of Accounts (COA), a foundational tool for organizing and recording transactions. This system acts as the backbone of your financial management, grouping data into categories for accurate reporting. Whether you're an accountant or a small business owner, having a well-structured COA ensures your financial records stay organized and easy to access.

This guide covers everything from understanding what the Chart of Accounts does to setting it up and customizing it to fit your business needs.

WHAT IS THE CHART OF ACCOUNTS IN QUICKBOOKS?

The Chart of Accounts (COA) in QuickBooks is a comprehensive list of all the accounts your business uses to track its financial activities. These accounts are categorized into:

- **Assets:** Resources owned by your business.
- **Liabilities:** Amounts owed to others.
- **Income**: Revenue earned by your business.
- **Expenses**: Costs incurred in running your business.
- **Equity:** The owner's stake in the business.

Each account plays a crucial role in financial reporting, providing insight into where your money is coming from, where it's going, and how it's being utilized. Think of the COA as a financial roadmap that guides you in managing your business effectively.

Setting Up the Chart of Accounts in QuickBooks Online

Here's how to get started with creating and customizing your Chart of Accounts in QuickBooks:

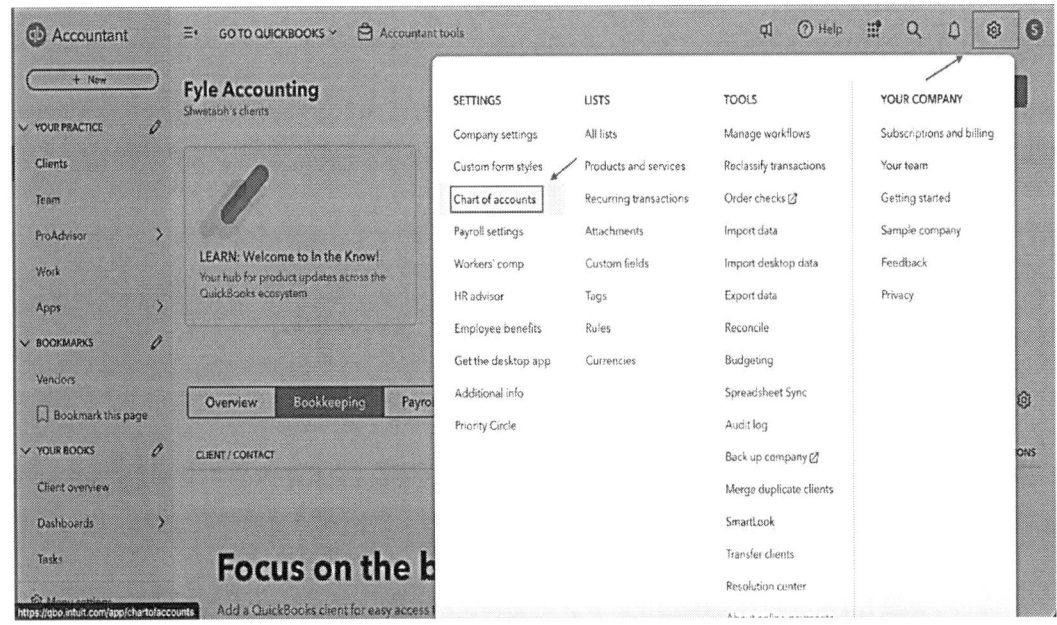

1. Click on the Settings icon located in the top-right corner of the screen.

2. From the drop-down menu, select Chart of Accounts.

On the Chart of Accounts page, ensure that all the necessary accounts are set up to align with your business workflows. This will allow you to categorize your transactions accurately and assign them to the appropriate accounts.

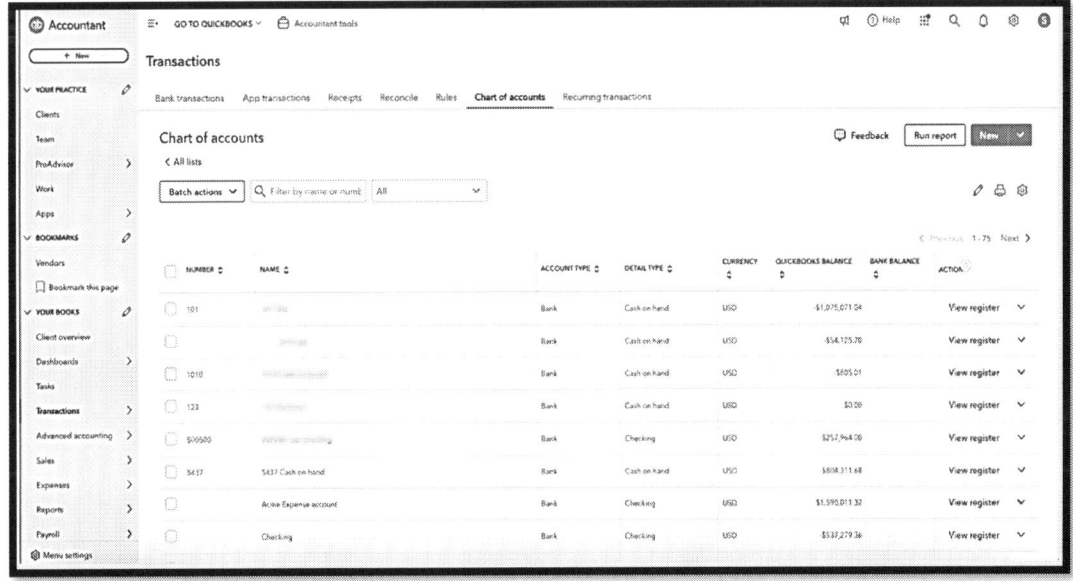

Scroll through your list of income accounts, and you'll notice default options like Billable Expense Income, Sales, and Services already included in QuickBooks Online. These standard accounts are built into the platform, but you can also create custom income accounts tailored to your business needs. For instance, a construction company might need specific income categories unique to its operations.

How to Add a New Account to Your Chart of Accounts

Step 1: On the Chart of Accounts page, click the new button to get started.

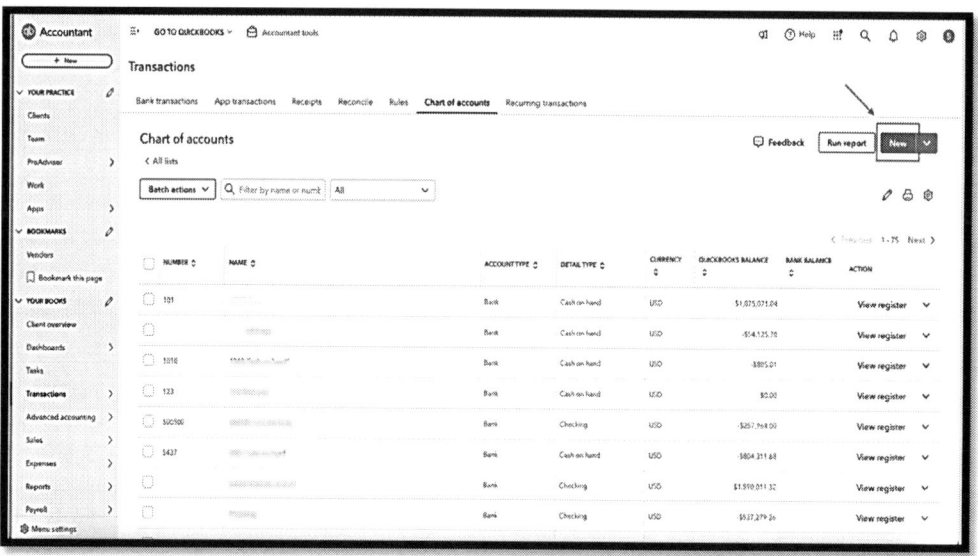

Step 2: A form will appear on the right side of your screen. Fill in the required fields to set up your new account. Below are the fields you'll need to complete, along with examples tailored to the construction industry:

1. Account Name

Purpose: This is the name of your new account. Choose a descriptive and easy-to-understand title.

  Example (Construction): "Construction Income"

2. Account Number

Purpose: A unique numeric code that helps you organize accounts and streamline financial reporting.

Example (Construction): "4000" (Create a numbering system that suits your business needs.)

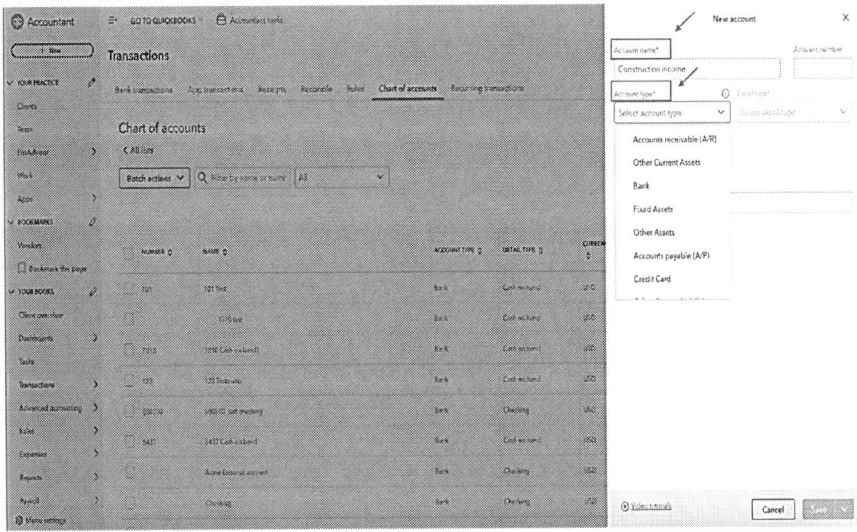

3. Account Type

Purpose: Categorizes the account for accurate financial analysis and reporting.

Example (Construction): "Income" or "Expense"

4. Detail Type

Purpose: Specifies the account's role within its category, allowing for more detailed financial tracking and insights.

Example (Construction): "Service/Fee Income" or "Discounts/Refunds Given"

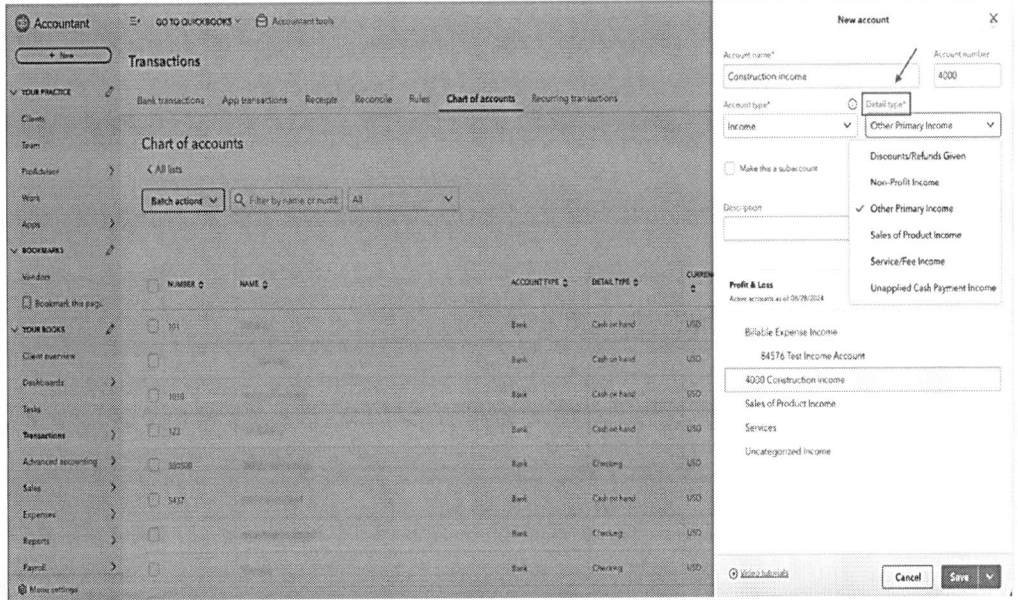

Step 3: Save Your New Account

Once you've filled out all the required fields, simply click "Save" to finalize the process.

Your newly created account will now appear in your Chart of Accounts. To locate it quickly, type the account name, such as "Construction," into the search bar. The account will instantly display in the list below for easy access.

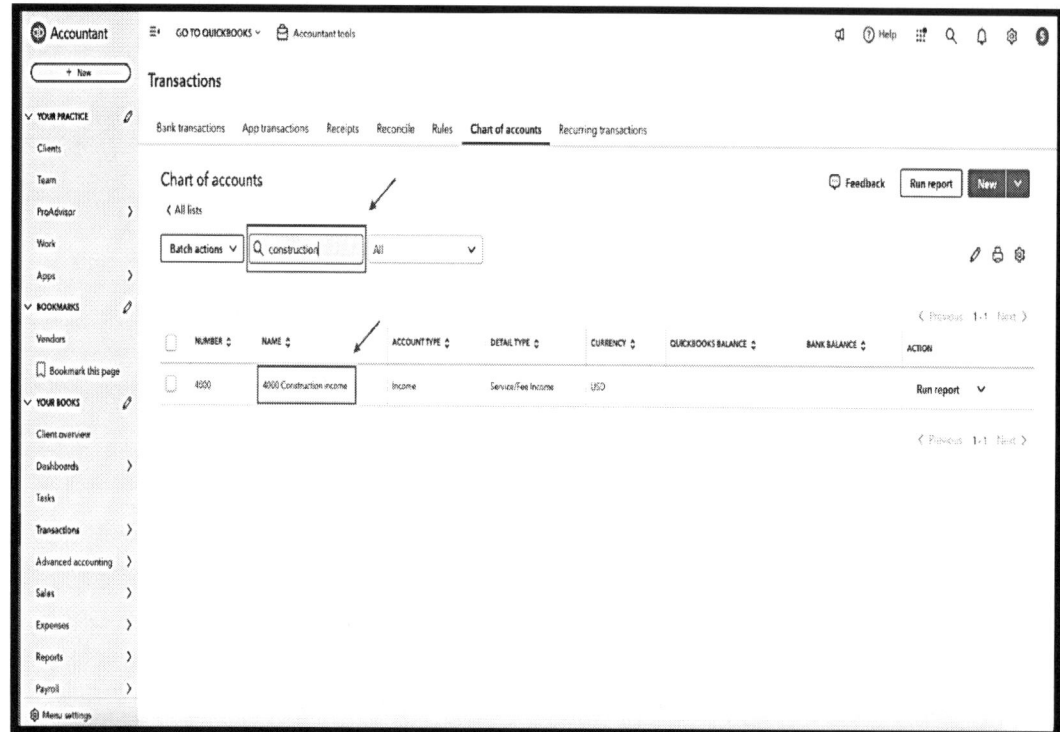

Simplifying Your QuickBooks Online Chart Accounts with flye

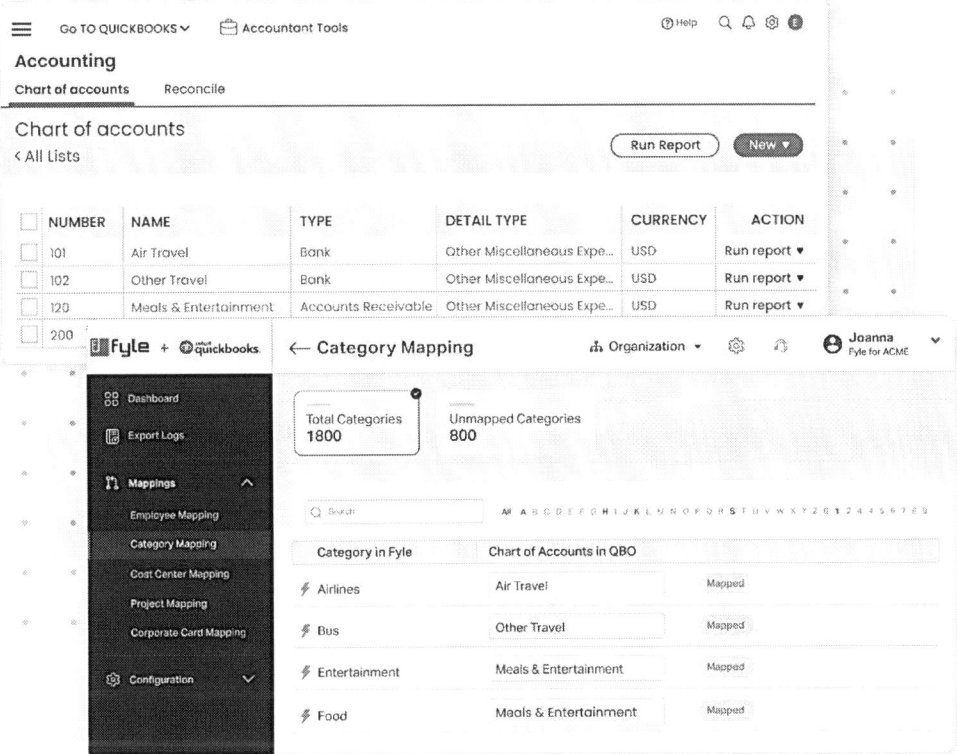

Fyle seamlessly integrates with QuickBooks Online to simplify expense categorization and organization. Here's how it enhances your experience with the Chart of Accounts (COA):

1. Automatic Account Import

Fyle automatically pulls Expense Accounts from QuickBooks Online's COA, eliminating manual data entry and ensuring expense categories in Fyle match those in QuickBooks.

2. Comprehensive Account Mapping

Fyle goes beyond Expense Accounts, allowing you to import account types such as Fixed Assets, Current Assets, Current Liabilities, Long-Term Liabilities, and Cost of Goods Sold (COGS). This flexibility enables you to map expenses based on your unique financial structure.

3. Simplified Account Naming

With Fyle, you can rename accounts or categories to simpler, more intuitive terms. This helps employees easily select the right accounts for their expenses without needing accounting expertise.

4. Custom Product and Service Mapping

Fyle lets you map Products and Services from QuickBooks Online to Fyle categories. This ensures a clear view of expenses tied to specific products or services, while guiding employees to accurately categorize their expenses.

5. Integration of Classes, Departments, and Projects

Fyle imports dimensions like Classes, Departments, and Projects from QuickBooks Online. Employees can then assign expenses directly to the relevant cost center or project with ease.

6. Control Over Account Mappings

You have full control over how accounts from QuickBooks Online are mapped to Fyle. Adjust mappings as needed to align with your business structure and ensure accurate categorization before exporting data back to QuickBooks.

7. Auto-Sync for Updates

Fyle syncs with QuickBooks Online every 24 hours, ensuring that any new accounts added in QuickBooks are automatically reflected in Fyle. This keeps both systems updated and in sync.

By streamlining integration with QuickBooks Online's COA, Fyle makes expense management and accounting accurate, efficient, and hassle-free.

DEACTIVATING AN ACCOUNT IN QUICKBOOKS ONLINE

Sometimes, you may need to deactivate an account in QuickBooks Online to better manage your books, whether due to changes in business structure or an account becoming obsolete. Here's how you can do it:

Step 1: Access the Chart of Accounts

From the "Transactions" menu, select the "Chart of Accounts" tab.

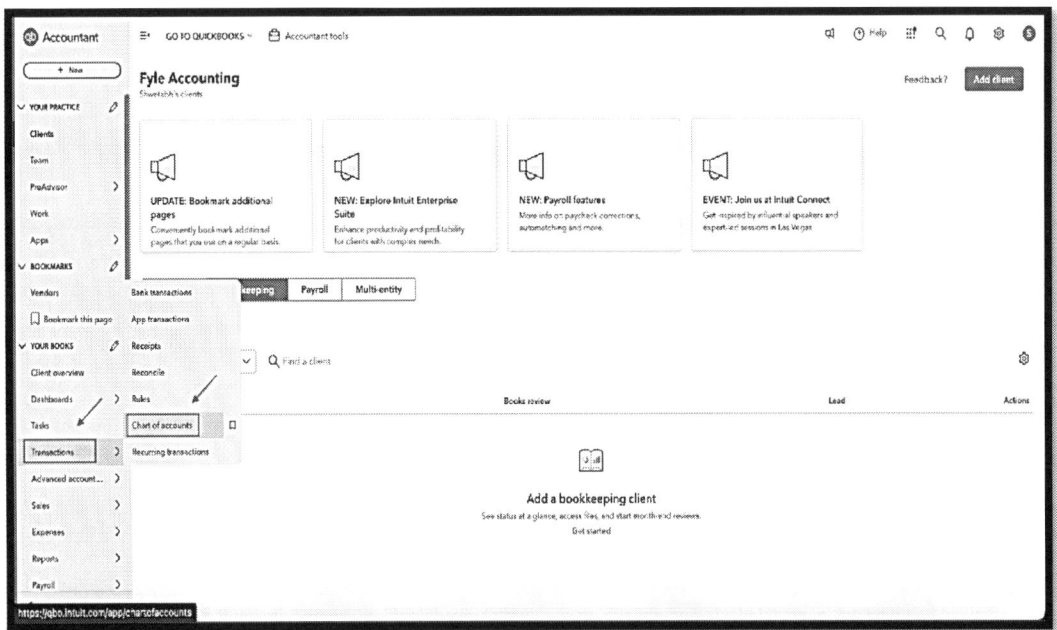

This will reveal all your accounts on screen.

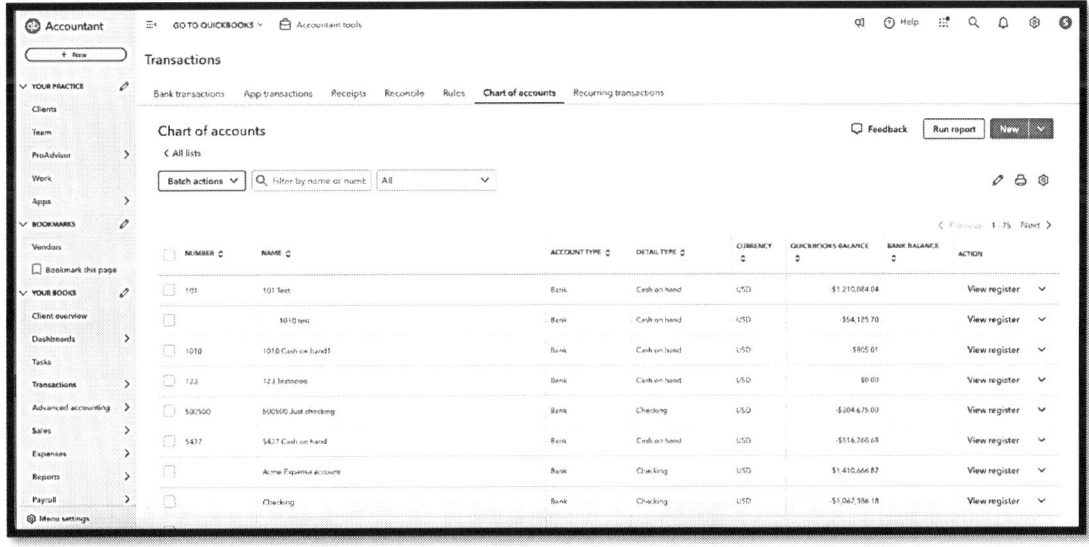

Step 2: Deactivate the Account

On the left side of the screen, find the account you wish to deactivate. Click on "Batch Actions" and then select "Make Inactive" to remove it from active use.

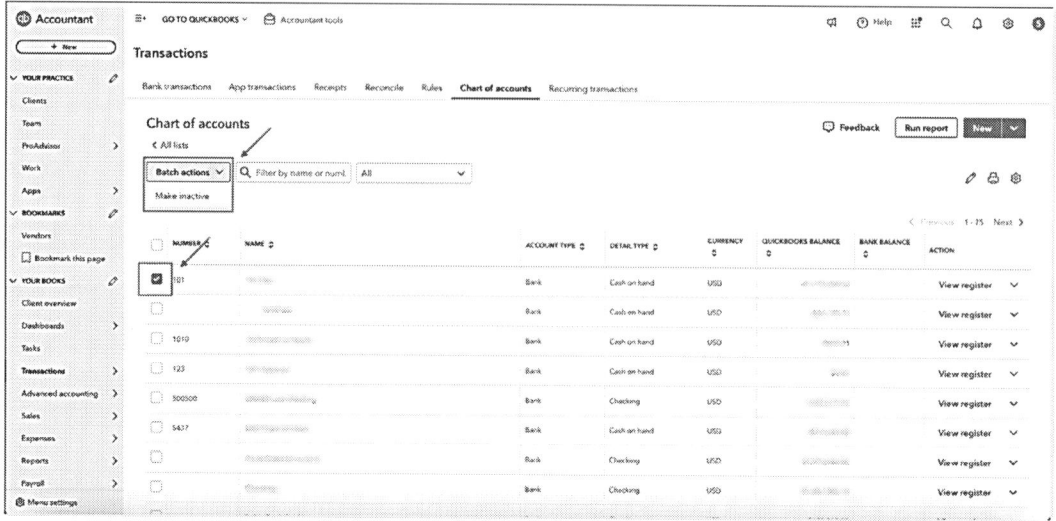

Step 3: Confirm Deactivation

Once you click "Make Inactive", a prompt will appear asking you to confirm your action. If you're sure, click "Yes, Make Inactive" to proceed.

That's it! You've successfully deactivated the account in QuickBooks Online. It will no longer appear as active in your Chart of Accounts but can still be reactivated later if needed.

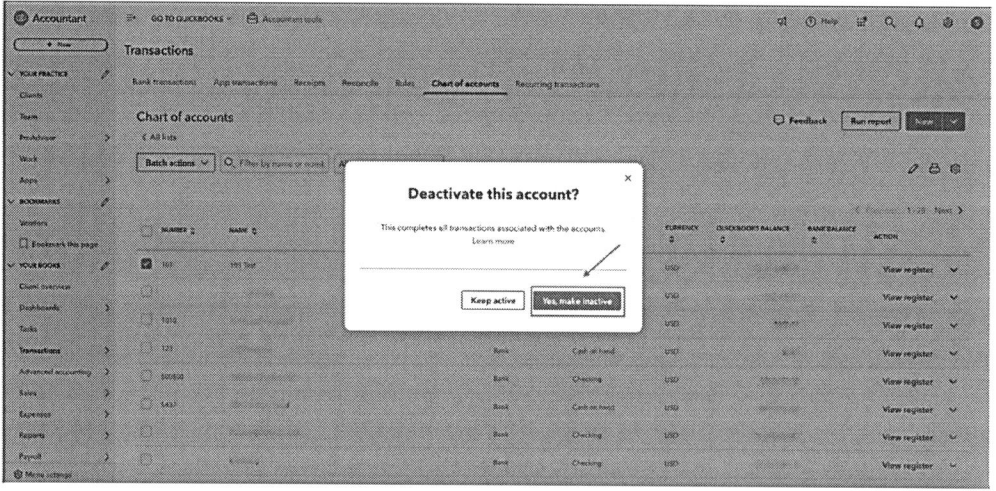

LINKING YOUR BANK AND CREDIT CARD ACCOUNTS SECURELY

Connecting your bank and credit card accounts to QuickBooks Online makes managing your finances simpler and more efficient. This feature ensures accurate records, automates transaction imports, and categorizes them for you. Here's a step-by-step guide to link your accounts securely:

1. Sign In to QuickBooks Online

Log in to your QuickBooks Online account using your credentials.

2. Access the Banking Section

Navigate to the left-hand menu and select "Banking" or "Transactions".

3. Add a Bank Account

Click on the "Link Account" or "Add Account" button.

4. Search for Your Bank

Use the search bar to find your bank or financial institution and select it from the list.

5. Enter Your Login Credentials

Input your online banking username and password to authorize QuickBooks to access your account.

6. Complete Authentication

Follow any additional security steps your bank requires, such as multi-factor authentication, to finalize the connection.

7. Choose Accounts to Connect

Select the specific bank or credit card accounts you want to link, enabling QuickBooks to start importing transactions.

8. Review and Confirm

Double-check the connection settings and confirm to begin syncing transactions automatically.

9. Categorize Transactions

Imported transactions will appear in the "For Review" tab within the Banking section. Review and categorize them to maintain accurate records.

10. Reconcile Your Account

Go to the "Accounting" menu and select "Reconcile". Follow the prompts to match your QuickBooks records with your bank statements, ensuring everything aligns perfectly.

By linking your bank and credit card accounts to QuickBooks Online, you can save time, improve accuracy, and keep your financial records up to date effortlessly.

HOW TO CONNECT CREDIT CARD ACCOUNTS TO QUICKBOOKS ONLINE

Connecting your credit card accounts to QuickBooks Online makes tracking and managing your financial transactions effortless. Follow these steps to link your credit card accounts:

Step-by-Step Process

1. Log In to QuickBooks Online

Access your QuickBooks Online account by entering your credentials.

2. Navigate to the Banking Section

From the left-hand menu, click on "Banking" or "Transactions".

3. Add a Credit Card Account

Click the "Link account" or "Add account" button to start the setup.

4. Search for Your Credit Card Provider

Use the search bar to enter the name of your credit card provider or bank, and choose the appropriate option from the results.

5. Enter Your Login Details

Provide your online banking credentials and complete any required security steps, such as two-factor authentication.

6. Select Accounts to Link

Pick the specific credit card accounts you wish to connect and begin syncing your transactions.

7. Confirm the Connection

Review the connection details and confirm to start importing transactions automatically.

8. Categorize Transactions

Go to the "For Review" tab in the Banking section to categorize and classify your transactions for accurate record-keeping.

9. Reconcile Your Credit Card Account

Under the "Accounting" menu, select "Reconcile", and follow the guided steps to match your credit card transactions with your statements.

TIPS FOR CONNECTING ACCOUNTS

- **Sync Regularly**: Keep your accounts up to date by syncing them frequently.
- **Secure Login Details:** Protect your online banking credentials and update them as needed.
- **Monitor Transactions**: Regularly review imported transactions to catch and correct any discrepancies.
- **Automate Categorization**: Use QuickBooks' categorization rules to save time and improve accuracy.

Conclusion

Connecting your credit card accounts to QuickBooks Online simplifies financial management. By following these straightforward steps, you can ensure your transactions are automatically imported, accurately categorized, and easily reconciled. This integration saves time, improves accuracy, and provides clear insights into your business's financial health.

FREQUENTLY ASKED QUESTIONS

1. What if my bank or credit card provider isn't listed in QuickBooks?

If your provider isn't listed, you can manually upload your transactions. Download them in formats like `.CSV`, `.QBO`, or `.QFX` from your bank's website and import them into QuickBooks.

2. How do I update my login credentials if they change?

Go to the Banking section, select the account to update, and follow the prompts to enter your new login information.

3. What should I do if transactions are missing or not syncing?

Check your connection settings and try syncing again. If the issue persists, contact QuickBooks support or your bank for assistance.

4. How can I disconnect a bank or credit card account in QuickBooks?

To disconnect an account, navigate to the Banking section, select the account, and choose the option to unlink or disconnect it.

5. How can I avoid duplicate transactions?

QuickBooks automatically detects duplicates. If any appear, you can exclude or delete them from the "For Review" tab.

AUTOMATING REPETITIVE TASKS TO SAVE TIME

When it comes to accounting, efficiency is key. But how do you ensure everything runs seamlessly, especially for an online business-like eCommerce? The answer lies in automation. By automating your accounting tasks, you can save time, reduce costs, and enhance the accuracy of your financial records.

Manual processes such as data entry and tax calculations are not only time-consuming but also prone to errors. While setting up automation may have initial hurdles, the long-term benefits far outweigh the challenges.

Key Takeaways

- Automating accounting tasks saves time, reduces costs, and improves accuracy.
- Automation ensures compliance with tax and payroll regulations globally.
- Although implementing automation can be challenging, the process is manageable with the right tools.

- Tasks such as bookkeeping, tax management, reporting, and expense tracking can be automated, prioritizing repetitive and time-intensive processes first.

For instance, tools like Link My Books enable eCommerce businesses to save an average of six hours a month on bookkeeping. Its Guided Tax Wizard ensures accurate tax calculations for each sale, while its reporting tools support business scaling.

So, where should you begin as an eCommerce business or accountant? This guide will walk you through the process of automating your accounting tasks step by step.

WHAT IS ACCOUNTING AUTOMATION?

Accounting automation involves using software to streamline various accounting tasks, making the process faster and more efficient. Instead of spending hours on manual work, automation tools handle these tasks instantly, improving accuracy and ensuring compliance with financial regulations.

Benefits of Accounting Automation

1. Save Time

The most apparent benefit of automation is the significant time savings. The more tasks you automate, the less time you or your team will spend on routine accounting processes.

For example:

- Automating eCommerce bookkeeping can save up to six hours per month.
- Extending automation to payroll, reporting, and tax calculations adds even more time savings.

2. Increase Accuracy

Manual tasks such as data entry, generating reports, and managing invoices are prone to errors. Even a small mistake, like a misplaced decimal point, can lead to costly consequences.

Automation helps eliminate such errors by:

- Ensuring tasks are completed with precision.
- Generating detailed and accurate reports that would be labor-intensive to create manually.

By embracing automation, businesses can enhance efficiency, reduce operational costs, and ensure their accounting remains compliant and error-free.

Stay Compliant

Staying compliant with tax and labor laws is essential for avoiding penalties and protecting your business's reputation. Automated accounting systems are regularly updated to reflect the latest tax laws and regulations. This ensures your business stays compliant without requiring you to constantly monitor changes or manually adjust calculations.

Save Money

While investing in automation software may seem like a significant upfront cost, it ultimately helps you save money. By reducing the time spent on manual accounting tasks, automation frees up resources for other important areas, such as marketing and customer engagement.

Additionally, automated systems minimize the need to hire external accountants for routine tasks. Instead, your in-house team and accountants can focus on more strategic activities like budget planning and developing business strategies.

AUTOMATE BOOKKEEPING

WHAT IS BOOKKEEPING?

Bookkeeping involves organizing and recording your financial transactions so that the information is easily accessible for tax filing or retrieving specific details. Effective bookkeeping ensures that your financial records are clear, accurate, and easy to manage.

Traditionally, bookkeeping was done manually using paper ledgers, spreadsheets, or accounting software. However, the advent of automated bookkeeping tools has significantly reduced the need for manual data entry, especially for eCommerce businesses and accountants.

Link My Books is an example of such a tool. It connects to your sales channels, automatically categorizes transactions, and transfers the data directly into your accounting system, saving you hours of effort each month.

Reconciliation

Reconciliation is the process of ensuring that your financial records align with your bank accounts and sales channels. While this task can be time-consuming, automation tools simplify the process by updating records automatically as transactions occur or when needed.

Modern accounting software can integrate directly with your bank, enabling real-time transaction recording. This ensures your books are always accurate and up to date.

Expense Management

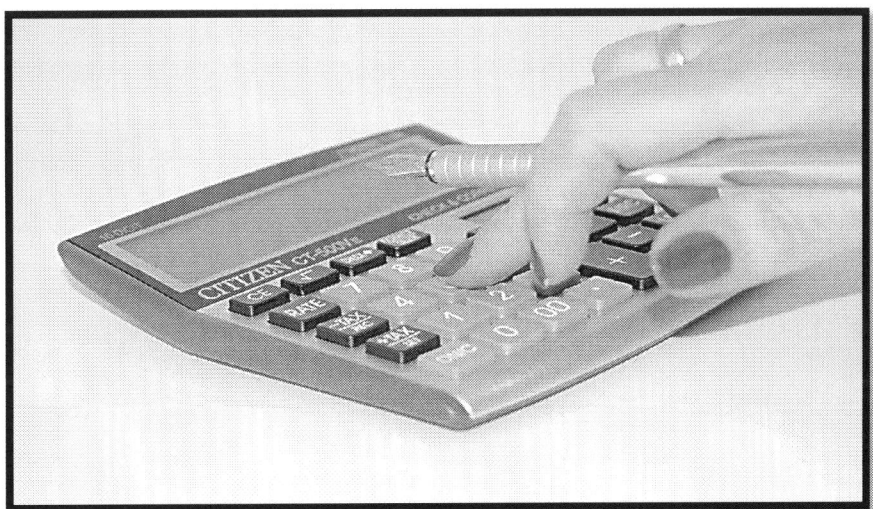

Expense Management

Managing expenses, especially when employees are involved, can be a complex and time-consuming process. Thankfully, automation tools simplify many aspects of expense management.

For instance, certain apps allow you to snap photos of receipts, automatically extracting and categorizing the data for you. Additionally, you can issue company cards with pre-set spending limits. All transactions made using these cards are automatically synced with your accounting software, ensuring seamless record-keeping.

Reporting and Analytics

Modern accounting software can generate essential reports, such as profit and loss statements or balance sheets, either on a schedule or upon request. These reports are created automatically based on the data in your system, eliminating the need for manual compilation.

Such reports are invaluable for making informed business decisions, as they highlight where money is being spent and which areas yield the best returns on investment. By automating reporting, you also reduce the risk of errors, ensuring more accurate and actionable insights.

Forecasting

Automation also enhances financial forecasting by leveraging historical data for trend analysis. These tools provide precise predictions about future financial outcomes, helping you make informed decisions and plan for your business's future with greater confidence.

Financial Forecasting

Accountants often face the challenging task of preparing financial forecasts, which requires analyzing both historical and current data. When done manually, this can be time-intensive and complex. However, with the right tools, cash flow, budget, and sales forecasts can be generated instantly and automatically. These forecasts use predefined formulas, making the process not only faster but also more accurate and reliable.

Accounts Receivable and Accounts Payable

Accounts Receivable (AR): This involves tasks such as creating and sending invoices, receiving customer payments, and reconciling accounts.

Accounts Payable (AP): Automating AP covers repetitive tasks like sending payment reminder emails, pre-filling invoices with accurate data, and reconciling payments received.

Automation in AR and AP improves cash flow by ensuring timely tracking of both incoming payments and outstanding balances. It minimizes delays between completing work and receiving payments, leading to smoother and more accurate financial management.

PAYROLL

Automation can significantly streamline payroll processes. Depending on the software, many payroll systems assist in ensuring compliance with employer obligations, such as calculating income tax, contributing to employee pensions, and keeping accurate payment records.

Some advanced payroll tools also offer a self-service portal for employees, allowing them to update personal information, request leave, and log working hours. This reduces administrative tasks for the employer and makes payroll management more efficient.

Tax Management

For eCommerce businesses operating across multiple regions, managing taxes for different jurisdictions can be complex and risky, with steep penalties for errors. Automated accounting tools simplify tax management by accurately calculating taxes for each jurisdiction and preparing tax returns.

These tools ensure your records are well-organized, regularly updated, and easy to access when filing taxes. This reduces errors and helps businesses stay compliant with tax regulations, even when operating internationally.

CHAPTER 3

STREAMLINING INVOICING AND PAYMENTS

As we step into 2025, the landscape of e-invoicing is evolving rapidly, driven by technological advancements and updated regulations. For small and medium-sized businesses (SMBs) and accounting professionals, staying informed about these changes is crucial for maintaining efficiency, ensuring compliance, and staying competitive in the market.

Top E-Invoicing Trends for 2025

1. AI and Machine Learning Leading the Way

Artificial Intelligence (AI) and Machine Learning (ML) are transforming e-invoicing, making processes smarter and more efficient:

- **Enhanced Automation:** AI-driven systems will manage complex tasks like anomaly detection, fraud prevention, and data validation with minimal manual input.
- **Predictive Insights**: Machine Learning will provide valuable forecasts, such as cash flow predictions, payment patterns, and potential compliance risks, empowering proactive decision-making.

- **Customized Invoicing:** AI will offer personalized invoicing experiences, tailoring communications and payment options to suit customer preferences and behavior.

2. Blockchain Ensuring Security and Transparency

Blockchain technology is redefining e-invoicing by adding unmatched security and transparency:

- **Immutable Records**: Invoices stored on the blockchain are tamper-proof, ensuring a trustworthy audit trail and minimizing fraud risks.
- **Smart Contracts**: Automated payments through smart contracts will speed up and enhance transaction accuracy.
- **Simplified Cross-Border Transactions**: Blockchain facilitates secure and unified verification for international invoicing, reducing complexities.

3. Growing Adoption of Cloud-Based Solutions

Cloud-based e-invoicing platforms are gaining popularity for their flexibility and cost-efficiency:

- **Remote Accessibility**: Businesses can manage invoices from anywhere, supporting hybrid work setups and global collaborations.
- **Effortless Scalability**: Cloud systems grow with the business, handling higher transaction volumes without requiring significant upgrades.
- **Centralized Data**: These platforms provide real-time data visibility and analytics on a single dashboard, simplifying decision-making.

4. Enhanced Interoperability and Standardization

Streamlined e-invoicing is becoming a reality through better compatibility and standardized practices:

- **Universal Standards:** Frameworks like UBL (Universal Business Language) and PEPPOL will foster easier integration across platforms and borders.
- **API Integration**: Improved APIs will enable seamless communication between e-invoicing tools, ERP systems, and regulatory platforms, boosting data accuracy and compliance.

5. Focus on Sustainability

Sustainability is becoming a central theme in e-invoicing, driven by environmental concerns and regulatory pressures:

- **Paperless Operations:** The shift from paper-based invoicing to digital processes will reduce waste and operational costs.
- **Green Compliance**: Businesses will adopt eco-friendly practices by adhering to regulations aimed at reducing carbon footprints through electronic documentation and reporting.

CREATING AND CUSTOMIZING PROFESSIONAL INVOICES

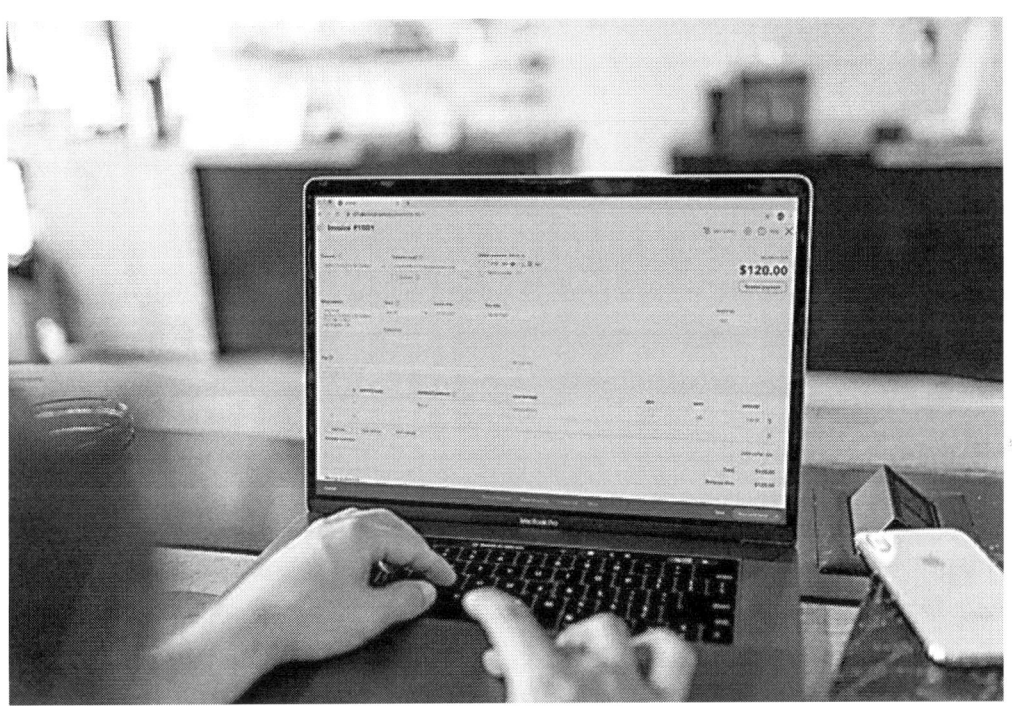

Why You Should Customize Your Invoices

Personalized invoices can significantly impact your small business. A professionally designed invoice with your company logo and an easy-to-read layout does more than simplify billing—it strengthens your brand image. Customers appreciate clarity and professionalism in their transactions.

Customizing your invoices in QuickBooks Online allows you to:

- Add branding elements like logos and colors that reflect your identity.

- Offer multiple payment options for a hassle-free experience.
- Make invoices easy to understand, ensuring smoother transactions.

Taking a little extra time to customize your invoices helps you stand out from competitors and shows your customers they're valued.

How to Get Started with Custom Invoices

If you're unsure how to customize invoices in QuickBooks Online or Desktop, you're in the right place. This guide will walk you through the best practices to create invoices that suit your business.

Additionally, tools like Method CRM expand your customization options, giving you even greater control over the look and functionality of your invoices.

Ready to elevate your invoicing? Read on for expert tips on customizing QuickBooks invoices and leveraging Method CRM for advanced features.

What is QuickBooks Online?

QuickBooks Online is a cloud-based accounting tool developed by Intuit. It's widely used by businesses to streamline financial management by organizing income and expenses.

One of its standout features is remote accessibility—you can manage your business finances from anywhere with an internet connection. Whether you're traveling or working from a café, QuickBooks Online ensures you stay in control of your company's financial health.

Curious about its features? Start your free trial of QuickBooks Online today!

Why Customized Invoices Matter

Custom invoices reflect professionalism and can elevate the customer experience while reinforcing your brand.

Here's why learning to customize invoices in QuickBooks Online and Desktop is essential:

1. Increase Brand Visibility

An invoice is more than just a payment request—it's a chance to make a lasting impression.

Custom invoices let you include details such as:

- Company logo
- Business name
- Contact information
- Return policies

These personalized elements create a memorable invoice that enhances brand recall and builds customer loyalty. When customers think about future purchases or recommendations, your branded invoice keeps your business top of mind.

By maintaining consistent branding, QuickBooks customization tools help create a professional and cohesive customer experience.

2. Add a Personal Touch

Today's customers value personalization. In fact, 84% of buyers prefer businesses that treat them as individuals rather than just another transaction.

Customizing your invoices lets you:

- Tailor communication to meet specific client preferences.
- Show appreciation by thanking customers personally and recognizing their importance to your business.
- Build trust by creating invoices that reflect care and professionalism.

QuickBooks simplifies the process, allowing you to design personalized, professional invoices that strengthen relationships and enhance customer loyalty.

Ready to impress your clients? Elevate your invoicing game with QuickBooks Online and Method CRM to create standout invoices that let customers know they're at the heart of your business.

Add a Personal Touch

Invoices don't have to feel transactional or impersonal. With a few simple tweaks, you can use QuickBooks to make your invoices reflect how much you value your customers.

Here are some ideas:

- **Personal notes**: Include a thank-you message or acknowledge their loyalty.
- **Exclusive offers**: Add a special discount for their next purchase to make them feel appreciated.

QuickBooks makes it easy to personalize invoices by letting you add customer names and unique details directly. This small gesture demonstrates that your business views customers as individuals, not just numbers.

MAKE YOUR INVOICES A VALUABLE RESOURCE

Why limit your invoice to just a list of transactions? Custom invoices can also serve as a helpful resource for your customers.

Consider including:

- Warranty expiration dates to remind customers of key timelines.
- Upcoming service appointments to keep them informed about scheduled services.

By adding this type of information, your invoices become more than just a bill—they become a useful document that customers will keep handy.

The Benefits:

- Customers associate positive feelings with your business when invoices provide value beyond the payment process.
- Important after-sales details are readily accessible, ensuring customer satisfaction.
- Automating these additions saves time internally while guaranteeing customers always have the information they need.

When you blend personalization with practical insights, your invoices transform into relationship-building tools that encourage repeat business.

HOW TO CUSTOMIZE YOUR QUICKBOOKS INVOICE: A SIMPLE GUIDE

If you're looking to update your QuickBooks invoice template, you're in the right place! This guide offers step-by-step instructions on how to create customized invoices in QuickBooks Online and Desktop.

You'll learn:

- How to personalize QuickBooks invoices.
- How to edit a QuickBooks invoice template.
- Steps to modify QuickBooks email templates.

Steps for QuickBooks Online Users

If you're a QuickBooks Online user and want to design a custom invoice, start with your company logo:

1. Navigate to the menu labeled "Account and Settings."

2. Click on the "Company" section.

3. Upload your company logo.

Adding your logo is the first step in creating professional, branded invoices that leave a lasting impression on your customers.

You can also upload your logo directly while customizing your invoices in the Design tab.

Here's how to get started:

1. Click the gear icon in the top-right corner of your QuickBooks screen.

2. Scroll down to the "Your Company" section and select "Custom Form Styles."

3. Choose "New Style" and then click "Invoice."

This process will guide you in creating a professional invoice design tailored to suit your business needs perfectly.

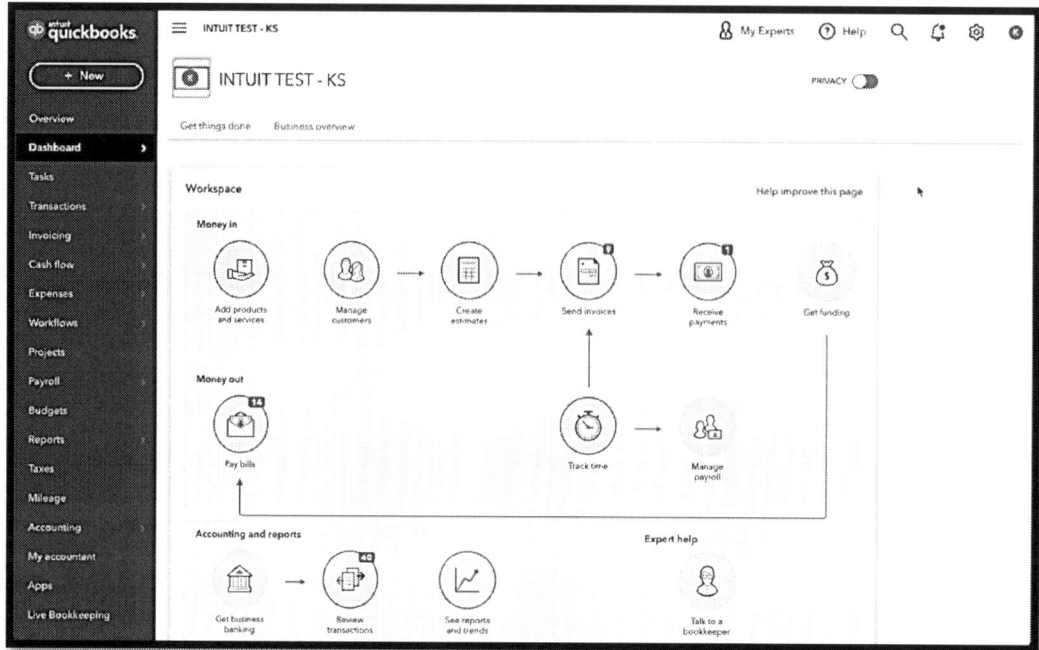

Customizing Invoices in QuickBooks Online

QuickBooks Online 2025 offers three straightforward ways to personalize your invoices:

1. Design: Add or update your logo, choose fonts, and select colors that align with your brand.

2. Content: Edit your business details, rename fields, and adjust column widths to better fit your needs.

3. Emails: Customize the email template sent with your invoices for a professional touch.

How to Customize an Invoice Template in QuickBooks Desktop

To modify an invoice template in QuickBooks Desktop:

1. Go to the "Lists" menu at the top of the screen.

2. Select "Templates."

3. Right-click the invoice template you wish to edit, then click "Edit Template."

This opens a customization window where you can:

- ○ Add your company logo.

- Select a color scheme and font style.
- Use the "Additional Customization" option to fine-tune fields—adding or removing specific details as needed.

⚠ Tip: Customized templates may not perfectly match QuickBooks' preprinted forms. To avoid issues, duplicate the default template before making edits.

Setting Up Recurring Invoices in QuickBooks Online

To automate invoicing in QuickBooks Online:

1. Click the gear icon in the upper-right corner.

2. Select "Recurring Transactions" and click "New."

3. Set the Transaction Type to Invoice and click "OK."

4. Change the Type to "Scheduled" and enable "Automatically send emails."

5. Complete the form with customer and transaction details, then save the template.

Once configured, recurring invoices will be automatically sent to your customers, saving you time and ensuring consistency in your billing process.

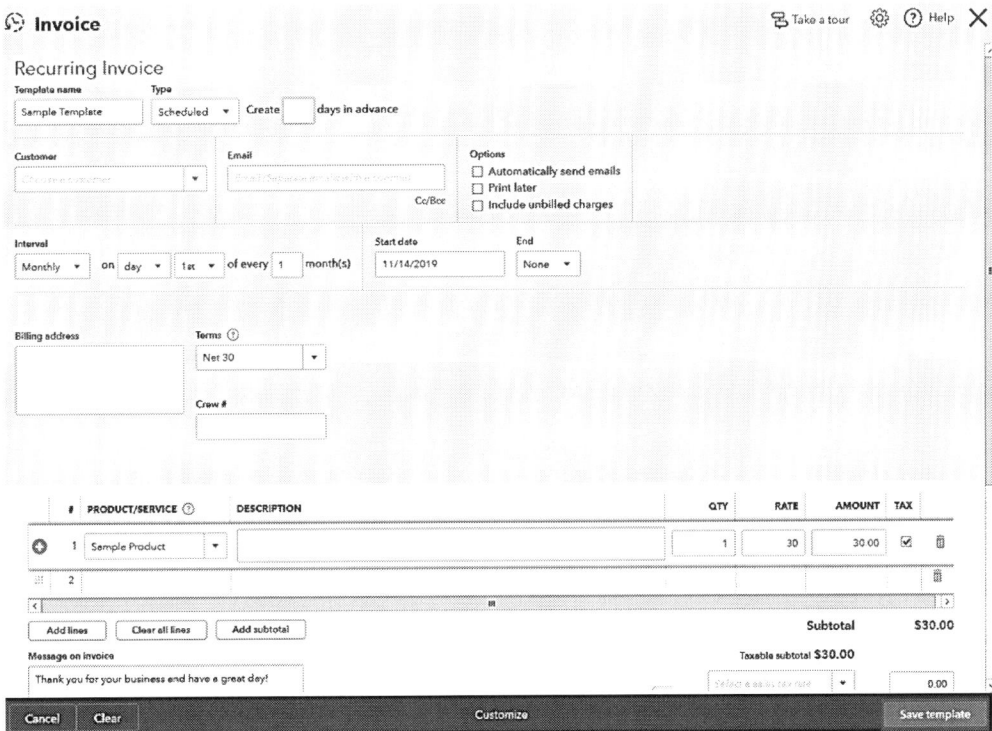

USING QUICKBOOKS DESKTOP FOR RECURRING INVOICES

To set up an invoice in QuickBooks Desktop:

1. Click "Quick Create" on the main screen, then select "Invoice."

2. Choose an existing customer or add a new one.

3. Fill out the necessary fields in the invoice form.

4. Toggle the online payment option to "On" for faster payment processing.

5. Once ready, click "Save and Send."

You'll need to follow these steps for each customer to establish recurring invoices, regardless of the QuickBooks version you use.

Efficiency Tip: While customizing invoices in QuickBooks Online and Desktop can save time and streamline billing, the process might feel repetitive. Stay tuned for insights on more efficient methods!

SETTING UP ONLINE PAYMENTS FOR FASTER TRANSACTIONS

Step 1: Sign Up or Link Your QuickBooks Payments Account

- If you don't already have a QuickBooks Payments account, sign up for one.
- Existing QuickBooks Payments users can link their account to QuickBooks Online by following the provided connection steps.

Step 2: Enable Online Payments in QuickBooks Online

Set Up Company Preferences:

1. Open Settings (gear icon) and click on Account and settings.

2. Navigate to the Payments section.

3. Under Chart of Accounts, click the Edit (pencil) icon.

4. Under Standard deposits, select the account where payments will be recorded.

5. For Processing fees, choose the expense account to track these fees.

   - Note: QuickBooks Solopreneur users cannot change the default expense account.

6. Click Save, then Done to apply your preferences.

Set Up Invoice Payment Settings:

1. Go to the Sales section.

2. Under Invoice payments, click the Edit (pencil) icon.

3. Select the payment methods (e.g., credit card, ACH) you want to offer customers.

4. Optionally, include payment instructions to display on invoices.

5. Click Save, then Done.

By enabling online payments, you streamline transactions and provide customers with a hassle-free way to pay.

SETTING PAYMENT OPTIONS ON INDIVIDUAL INVOICES

You can customize payment options for individual invoices without altering your company-wide preferences. Here's how:

Updating Payment Options on Invoices

For the Old Invoicing System

1. Navigate to Sales and select Invoices.

2. Find the invoice you want to update and click Edit.

3. In the Online payments section, adjust the payment options as needed.

4. Click Save or Save and close.

Optional: To email the invoice:

- Click Save and send.
- In the review window, update the subject line and email body with relevant details.
- Click Send and close.

For the New Invoicing System

1. Go to the Sales section and select Invoices.

2. Click Edit next to the invoice you wish to update.

3. In the Online payments section, select Edit to modify the payment methods.

4. Use the toggle switches to turn specific payment options on or off.

5. Click Save or Save and close.

Optional: To send the invoice via email:

- Click Save and send.
- Review the email in the preview window and add any necessary details.
- Click Send and close.

By customizing payment options at the invoice level, you can tailor the payment experience to suit each customer's needs while maintaining flexibility.

PROCESSING PAYMENTS IN QUICKBOOKS ONLINE

Now that you're ready to receive payments, here's how to process them depending on your customer's payment method.

Note: Payments will be deposited into the bank account linked during your QuickBooks Payments setup. For details on deposit timelines, refer to the QuickBooks Payments deposit speeds article.

Processing Sales Receipts for Payments

If a customer pays in person and doesn't require an invoice, create a sales receipt:

1. Click + New, then select Sales receipt.

2. From the Customer dropdown, choose an existing customer or click + Add new to create a new one.

   Tip: Add the customer's email to automatically send them a copy of the receipt.

3. Under Payment method, select how the customer paid.

For credit card payments using a card reader, click Enter credit card details, then select Swipe card.

4. In the PRODUCT/SERVICE field, choose the relevant item.

 If it's not listed, click + Add new to add a product or service.

5. Once all details are complete, click Save or Save and close.

PROCESSING PAYMENTS FOR INVOICES

If you've already issued an invoice and the customer pays in person:

1. Encourage the customer to use the payment link in their email for online payment.

  - If they prefer to pay directly in person:

2. Click + New and then choose Receive payment.

3. Under Customer, select the customer or click + Add new to create one.

4. Specify the Payment date.

5. Enter the payment details, including the Reference number and Amount received.

6. In the Deposit to field, select the account where the payment will be recorded.

7. From the dropdown, select the Payment method.

  For credit card payments using a card reader, select Enter credit card details.

8. In the Outstanding Transactions section, highlight the invoice being paid.

  For partial payments, input the amount received in the PAYMENT field.

9. Click Save and close or save and new.

These steps help ensure your payments are recorded accurately and efficiently, no matter how your customer chooses to pay.

Printing Receipts

When customers pay online, they automatically receive an email receipt. If you need a printed copy:

1. Go to Sales and select Invoices.

2. Open the Paid invoice, then click Receive payment for the transaction you need a receipt for.

3. Click Print and choose either Print or Download.

Note: Payment services are provided by Intuit Canada Payments Inc.

MANAGING OVERDUE INVOICES AND CLIENT FOLLOW-UPS

What Is a Past-Due Invoice?

A past-due invoice is a bill that remains unpaid after the payment deadline outlined in your terms. Late payments can disrupt your cash flow, making it harder to meet your financial obligations. While following up on overdue invoices can feel daunting, staying calm and professional is key to resolving the situation and getting paid.

HOW TO FOLLOW UP ON PAST-DUE PAYMENTS

1. Set Clear Payment Expectations from the Start

Before starting any project, discuss payment preferences with your client to prevent delays. If it's too late for your current project, this is a great tip for future work.

Two key points to clarify:

Recipient of the invoice: Should the invoice go directly to the client, their accounting department, or both? This ensures smoother processing and faster payments.

Preferred payment method: Offer flexible options like credit cards, eChecks, or ACH transfers to minimize delays caused by inconvenient methods.

For instance, a client accustomed to paying by credit card might face delays if asked to mail a check. A simple question like, "Would another payment method work better for you?" can save time and frustration.

2. Ensure Your Invoice is Clear and Comprehensive

Clients are more likely to pay on time if they fully understand the charges. Make sure your invoice includes:

- Consultation time
- Hours worked on tasks
- Research or project preparation
- Specific deliverables tied to project numbers
- Material costs

If you don't already have one, create a catalog of your services or products. This will make invoicing and future operations more efficient.

Tip: Clearly outline payment terms and due dates to avoid ambiguity. Instead of vague phrases like "immediate payment," use terms like "Net 30" (payment due within 30 days).

To further encourage on-time payments, send friendly reminders a week before the due date. A quick email nudge can prompt action and help you avoid late payments.

3. Set Up a Follow-Up System for Overdue Payments

Addressing late payments can feel intimidating, especially if it impacts your ability to pay your own bills. A structured system for handling overdue invoices can make the process less stressful and keep interactions professional.

Benefits of accounting software:

- Organizes invoices by client name or due date.
- Sends automated reminders for overdue payments.

Unlike manual methods like Excel or Word, accounting software streamlines the process, saving you time and helping you maintain timely follow-ups.

By implementing these strategies, you can efficiently manage overdue invoices while maintaining strong client relationships.

HOW TO WRITE A PAYMENT REMINDER LETTER

When sending a reminder about an overdue payment, ensure your letter includes all the necessary details to make it clear and actionable:

1. Invoice Number: Reference the specific invoice to avoid confusion.

2. Invoice Issue Date: Establish the timeline of the transaction.

3. Due Date: Clearly state when the payment was due.

4. Payment Terms: Specify arrangements like "Net 30" or any other agreed terms.

5. Amount Owed: Include any applicable late fees.

6. Payment Instructions: Provide details for bank transfers or links for online payments.

7. Your Contact Information: Add your email or phone number for questions or clarification.

Including these details ensures your customer can easily understand and resolve the overdue payment.

To make the process smoother, consider using automation tools like QuickBooks to send payment reminders. If automation isn't an option, prepare a professional and friendly payment reminder template to communicate effectively.

TRACKING SALES TAX HASSLE-FREE

What is Sales Tax?

Sales tax is a government-imposed fee on the sale of goods and services, typically collected at the point of purchase. The seller is responsible for collecting the tax from the buyer and remitting it to the government.

Who Pays Sales Tax?

The ultimate consumer—the person who uses the final product—generally bears the cost of sales tax. Transactions along the supply chain may not always be subject to this tax. For example:

- If you buy wool to produce blankets for resale, you typically won't pay sales tax on the wool.
- In such cases, you can avoid tax by providing a government-issued certificate verifying that your purchase is for manufacturing or resale.

SALES TAX RULES VARY BY JURISDICTION

Sales tax regulations depend on where you operate. Some factors to consider include:

- **Location-Based Taxation**: You may need to calculate state, city, or county taxes depending on your jurisdiction.
- **Usage-Based Taxation:** Sometimes, taxes depend on where the product will be used. For example, if you buy a car in one state but plan to register it in another, you'll pay sales tax based on the state where the car will be registered.

Understanding sales tax rules can be complex, so staying informed about local regulations is crucial for compliance and smooth business operations.

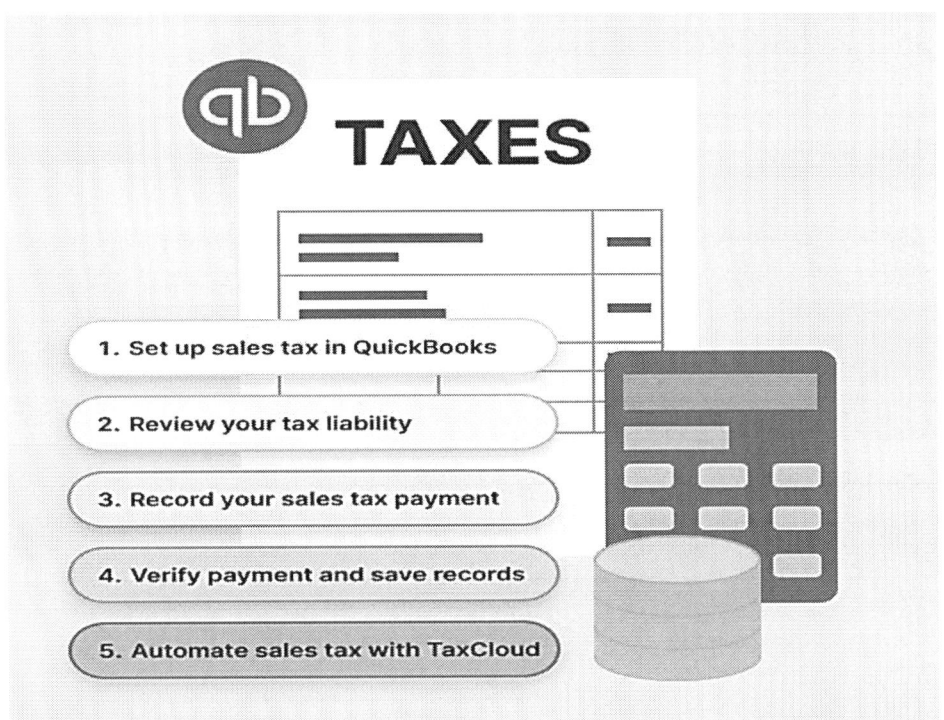

Did you know there were 780 changes to U.S. sales tax regulations in 2014 alone? It's no wonder many businesses find managing sales tax overwhelming. Handling sales tax manually is not only time-consuming but also increases the risk of errors and potential penalties.

The solution? Automate your sales tax process with QuickBooks Online. It makes collecting, reporting, and remitting sales taxes straightforward. For even greater efficiency, consider using TaxCloud, a powerful sales tax automation tool.

WHY USE TAXCLOUD WITH QUICKBOOKS ONLINE?

TaxCloud enhances your sales tax workflow by:

- Automatically calculating tax rates based on sales locations.
- Generating accurate, error-free tax reports.
- Filing sales tax returns directly from the platform.

Bonus: You can try TaxCloud free for 30 days to see how it simplifies compliance.

HOW TO PAY SALES TAX IN QUICKBOOKS ONLINE

Step 1: Set Up Sales Tax in QuickBooks Online

Start by enabling automated sales tax calculations in QuickBooks:

1. Open Taxes from the left-hand menu and choose Sales Tax.

2. Activate the Automated Sales Tax feature to allow QuickBooks to calculate taxes based on customer locations.

3. Set your business location for accurate tax application.

FOR ADVANCED AUTOMATION

- Create a TaxCloud account and connect it to QuickBooks Online.
- Assign sales tax items to your products and services, ensuring proper classifications to avoid errors.

Integrating TaxCloud with QuickBooks saves time, minimizes errors, and keeps you compliant effortlessly.

Step 2: Review Your Sales Tax Liability

Regularly reviewing your sales tax liability ensures compliance and accuracy. QuickBooks generates reports showing how much tax you owe. To review:

1. Navigate to the Taxes section in QuickBooks.

2. Click Sales Tax to view your liability report.

3. Check key details like:

- Taxable and non-taxable sales.
- Total tax collected during the reporting period.

If you're using TaxCloud, liability reports are generated automatically, ensuring precise tax rates based on customer locations—especially useful for businesses operating in multiple jurisdictions.

STEP 3: RECORD SALES TAX PAYMENT IN QUICKBOOKS ONLINE

After paying sales tax through your state's portal, record the payment in QuickBooks to keep your books accurate:

1. Go to Taxes > Sales Tax to open the Sales Tax Center.

2. Locate the return period for your payment.

3. Review the tax return using the View Tax Return option.

4. Click Record Payment and fill in:

- Payment amount.
- Payment date.
- Bank used for payment.

Double-check your details, save the entry, and ensure your liability account is updated.

Step 4: Verify Payment and Save Records

Once the payment is complete, confirm it with your state agency and maintain accurate records:

1. Check for a Confirmation Email: Keep the receipt as proof of payment for audits.

2. Record in QuickBooks: Attach the receipt to the transaction using QuickBooks' Attachments feature.

3. Automate with TaxCloud: TaxCloud automatically generates payment records and reports, streamlining audit preparation.

Step 5: Automate Sales Tax Management with TaxCloud

TaxCloud simplifies sales tax management in the following ways:

- **Automatic Calculations**: Computes sales tax based on product type and buyer location, ensuring accuracy.
- **Comprehensive Reports:** Provides detailed summaries of taxable sales, taxes collected, and amounts owed.
- **Seamless Filing and Payment**: File and pay taxes directly through TaxCloud.
- **Nexus Tracking**: Monitors your sales activities and alerts you when you create a nexus in another state, helping you avoid penalties.

By integrating TaxCloud with QuickBooks, you can save time, reduce errors, and maintain full compliance with ease.

CHAPTER 4
MANAGING EXPENSES AND BILLS

Keep your business finances in order by managing and tracking your bills effectively. Here's how you can do it in QuickBooks Online:

Step 1: Sign In to Your Account

1. Go to the Expenses menu.

2. Select Bills to access your bill management page.

Step 2: Navigate the Bills Page

The Bills page is organized into three main tabs:

For Review: Contains bills that need your attention.

Open a bill, verify its details, and save it to move it to the Unpaid tab.

Unpaid: Displays outstanding bills categorized by their status:

- Due later: Bills not yet due.
- Due soon: Bills nearing their due date.
- Overdue: Bills past their due date.
- Use the Mark as Paid option for bills paid outside of QuickBooks.
- Paid: Lists settled bills and linked payments. Click on a bill to view its details.

ADDING BILLS TO QUICKBOOKS

Manually Enter a Bill

If you receive a bill from a supplier, you can manually record it in QuickBooks:

1. Go to + New and select Bill.

2. In the Supplier dropdown, choose the supplier's name.

3. Specify the bill's Terms (e.g., Net 30), which indicate when payment is due.

4. Enter the Bill date, Due date, and Bill number from the invoice.

5. Under Category details:

- Select the Expense account for tracking.

- Add a brief description of the expense.

Tip: To itemize the bill (e.g., specific products or services), enable this feature in Settings:

- Go to Settings ⚙ > Account and settings > Expenses.
- Turn on Show Items table on expense and purchase forms.

6. Enter the total Amount and any applicable VAT.

7. If the expense is billable to a customer, check the Billable box and select the customer's name.

8. Click Save and close.

Manually entered bills will go directly to the Unpaid tab without further review.

UPLOAD BILLS FROM YOUR COMPUTER

If you have digital copies of your bills, you can upload them directly to QuickBooks:

1. Go to Expenses > Bills.

2. Click Add bill ▼ and select Upload from computer.

3. Drag and drop the bill file into the upload window, or click Upload to browse your files.

   Supported formats: PDF, JPEG, JPG, GIF, and PNG.

4. Uploaded bills appear in the For Review tab. Confirm the details and decide whether to pay now or later.

Recording Bill Payments

If you haven't paid a bill yet, you can:

- Schedule the payment for later.
- Record payments made through cheque, cash, or credit card.

Accurately recording payments ensures your financial records stay up-to-date.

By following these steps, you'll be able to efficiently manage, track, and settle bills in QuickBooks Online, helping you stay organized and maintain accurate financial records.

RECORDING EXPENSES AND UPLOADING RECEIPTS IN A SNAP

Uploading Receipts and Bills to QuickBooks Online

You can make tracking and recording of your supplier receipts and bills easier by uploading them to QuickBooks Online. You can upload from your computer, mobile device, or even email.

HOW IT WORKS

When you upload a receipt or bill, QuickBooks automatically extracts essential details and creates a transaction for your review. You can then:

- Edit the transaction details as needed.
- Assign it to the appropriate account.
- Match it to an existing transaction in the Receipts tab.

Tip: If you require employees to upload receipts for expense claims, consider upgrading to QuickBooks Online Advanced. This feature simplifies reviewing and matching their claims.

Before You Start

Keep these points in mind before uploading receipts or bills:

1. Avoid Sensitive Information:

Do not upload receipts or bills containing personal or sensitive details, such as credit card numbers or government-issued IDs.

2. Supported File Formats:

QuickBooks accepts these file types: PDF, JPEG, JPG, GIF, and PNG.

If you're using a newer iPhone or iPad, images may be in HEIC format. Convert them to a compatible format before uploading.

3. Currency Limitations:

The Receipt Snap feature only supports transactions in your home currency and does not work with multiple currencies.

STEP 1: UPLOAD YOUR RECEIPTS AND BILLS

There are multiple ways to upload receipts and bills to QuickBooks Online. Choose the method that works best for you:

1. From Your Computer:

- Log in to QuickBooks Online.

- Click on Receipts in the Expenses menu.
- Upload files directly from your computer.

2. Using Your Mobile Device:

- Open the QuickBooks mobile app.
- Go to the Receipts tab and use your phone's camera to capture an image of the receipt or bill.

3. From Email:

- Forward the email containing the receipt or bill attachment to your unique QuickBooks email address.
- QuickBooks will extract the data and display it under the Receipts tab for your review.

Uploading your receipts and bills into QuickBooks Online saves you significant time and eliminates manual data entry. Let QuickBooks handle the extraction and organization, ensuring accurate expense management.

As your business grows, you can upgrade to QuickBooks Online Advanced for features like employee expense submissions, further streamlining your processes.

UPLOADING RECEIPTS AND BILLS TO QUICKBOOKS ONLINE

Keeping track of your receipts and bills in QuickBooks Online is simple and efficient. You can upload them from your computer, mobile device, or email. Here's how:

Upload Receipts or Bills from Your Computer

1. Sign In: Log in to your QuickBooks Online account.

2. Navigate: Go to the Transactions menu and select Receipts.

3. Upload: Click Upload from computer to add your files.

   Note: Each file or image should contain only one receipt or bill.

Snap a Photo of Receipts or Bills with Your Mobile Device

If you prefer using your smartphone, the QuickBooks Online mobile app allows you to take photos and upload receipts or bills directly.

Step-by-Step Guide:

1. Install the App: Make sure the QuickBooks Online mobile app is installed on your iOS or Android device.

2. Open the App:

- Tap the Menu ≡ icon.
- Select Receipt snap.

3. Take a Photo:

- Tap the Camera icon to take a photo of your receipt or bill.
- Tap Use this photo, then tap Done.

Tip: On Android devices, you can disable the shutter sound for taking photos by adjusting your phone settings.

Email Receipts or Bills to QuickBooks

You can also email receipts or bills directly to QuickBooks Online, letting QuickBooks extract the details for you.

1. Email the receipt or bill to your designated QuickBooks email address.

2. QuickBooks will process the attachment, extract the details, and create a transaction for you to review.

Step 2: Review, Add, or Match Receipts and Bills

Once receipts and bills are uploaded, they don't automatically appear in your records. You'll need to review them, make edits, add new entries, or match them with existing transactions.

You can do this easily on both the web browser and the QuickBooks mobile app to ensure your financial records are accurate and up to date.

By using QuickBooks Online, you can efficiently upload, organize, and manage your receipts and bills, whether through your computer, mobile device, or email. This keeps your records accurate and saves time managing expenses.

MANAGING RECEIPTS AND BILLS IN QUICKBOOKS ONLINE

Keeping your financial records organized in QuickBooks Online is easy. Whether you use a web browser or a mobile app, here's how you can review, match, or add receipts and bills to your books.

On a Web Browser

1. Access Receipts

Go to the Transactions menu and select Receipts.

2. Review the "For Review" Tab

- o   This tab lists all uploaded receipts and bills that need attention.
- o   QuickBooks may highlight potential matching transactions already in your records.

3. Take Action Based on Matches

No Match Found: If QuickBooks can't find a match:

1. Click Review to edit or add missing details.

2. Click Save and next.

3. Choose Create bill or Create expense to add the transaction to your books.

One Match Found: If QuickBooks finds a matching transaction:

1. Click Match to link it directly.

2. If you want to review before matching, click the dropdown (▼) next to Match and select Review.

3. Edit details if needed, click Save and next, and confirm the match.

Multiple Matches Found: If there are two or more possible matches:

1. Click Review.

2. Compare the potential matches and choose the correct one.

3. Select Match to finalize.

ON AN IOS OR ANDROID DEVICE

1. Open the QuickBooks Mobile App

Tap the Menu ≡ icon and choose Receipt snap.

2. Review the "For Review" Tab

- This tab shows receipts and bills not yet added to your books.
- Labels under the receipt/bill amount indicate what needs to be done.

3. Handle Matches and Missing Details

If Matches Are Found:

1. Tap the receipt to view matching transactions.

2. Select the correct transaction to match.

If No Match Found (No Label):

1. Tap the receipt or bill.

2. Choose Create expense or Create bill to add it manually.

Tip: Swipe left or right on the receipt to quickly add it as an expense or bill.

If Details Are Missing:

1. Tap the receipt or bill.

2. Enter any required details manually and select Save receipt or Save bill.

3. Create the corresponding transaction.

4. Track Reviewed Items

- Once receipts or bills are added to your books, they move to the Reviewed tab.
- To unmatch an item and return it to the For Review tab, swipe right on the receipt or bill.

Keep Your Records Accurate

By following these steps, you'll ensure all your receipts and bills are correctly recorded in QuickBooks Online, whether using a web browser or mobile app. This keeps your books up to date and your financial records organized.

SETTING UP VENDOR PROFILES FOR SEAMLESS PAYMENTS

Managing vendor payments is simple and efficient with QuickBooks, whether you're using QuickBooks Online or QuickBooks Desktop. Here's how to set it up and pay vendors with ease.

Paying Vendors with QuickBooks: Online and Desktop

QuickBooks streamlines vendor payments, but there are differences between the Online and Desktop versions:

- **QuickBooks Online:** Offers Online Bill Pay through a third-party service (requires a separate subscription).
- **QuickBooks Desktop**: Includes vendor payment features without needing a third-party service.

Key Steps for Vendor Payments

1. **Activate ACH Bank Transfers**: Set up electronic bank transfers for your vendors.

2. **Create Vendor Credits:** Use credits to offset vendor payments.

3. **Pay by Check Before Verification**: Issue checks before your bank account is fully verified.

4. **Choose Your Payment Method:** Pay vendors using checks or ACH transfers.

USING ONLINE BILL PAY IN QUICKBOOKS ONLINE

While QuickBooks Online offers Online Bill Pay, some limitations exist:

- **Recurring Payments**: Not supported directly in Online Bill Pay, but you can set up bill reminders to avoid missing payments.
- **Vendor Credits:** Credits do not automatically sync with Online Bill Pay.
- **Advanced Features**: For options like multiple payment methods or automated approvals, consider third-party apps integrated with QuickBooks Online.

For accounting professionals, QuickBooks Online Accountant allows CPAs and bookkeepers to connect advanced third-party bill payment apps to each client's QuickBooks account for added flexibility.

How to Pay Vendors in QuickBooks Online

Paying vendors in QuickBooks Online is straightforward, with automatic bill creation in the background. Here's how:

1. Access the Dashboard:

Log in to your QuickBooks Online account and navigate to the dashboard.

2. Open Bill Pay Online:

Click the Bill pay online widget.

3. Make a Payment:

Select the Make a payment tab and follow the prompts to complete the payment.

Enhance Vendor Payments with Third-Party Apps

For additional features like recurring payments or automated workflows, explore third-party apps compatible with QuickBooks Online. These integrations can streamline your payment processes, making them more efficient and flexible.

By setting up vendor profiles and utilizing QuickBooks' payment tools, you'll keep your finances organized and ensure timely payments to your vendors.

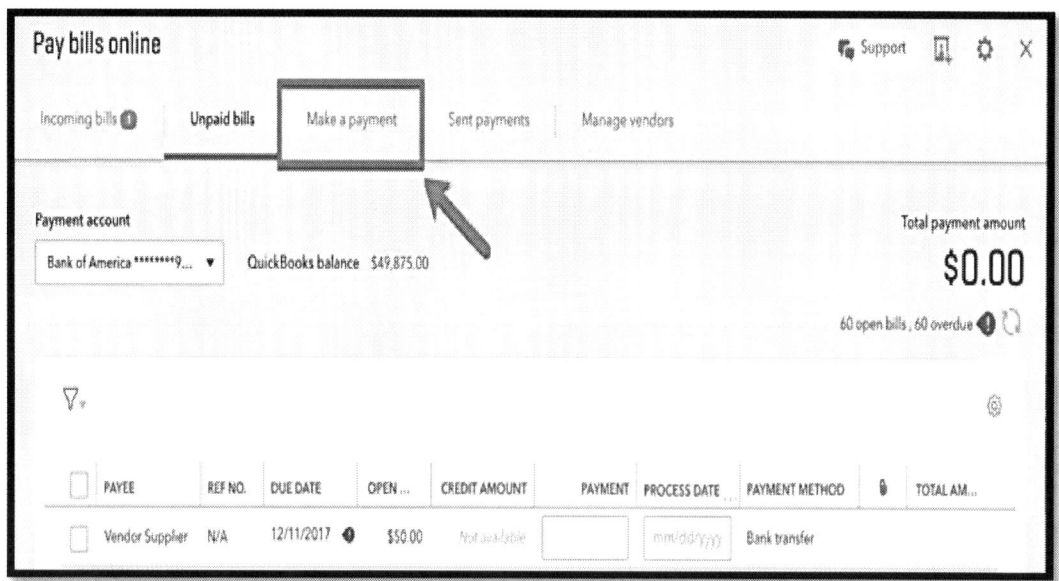

ENTERING VENDOR PAYMENT INFORMATION IN QUICKBOOKS

When recording a payment for a vendor in QuickBooks, make sure to include the necessary details to ensure accuracy and proper tracking.

Required Payment Details

The payment entry should include:

- **Vendor Name:** Identify the recipient of the payment.
- **Payment Amount**: Specify the total amount being paid.
- **Memo (optional):** Add any relevant notes about the payment.
- **Bill Number**: Reference the invoice or bill number for easy tracking.
- **Payment Account**: Indicate the account from which the payment is made.
- **Account:** Choose the correct account from your chart of accounts.
- **Description:** Provide a brief explanation of the payment, if necessary.
- **Customer (if applicable):** Link the payment to a customer if it's related.
- **Class (if applicable):** Assign a class for tracking purposes.

Selecting the Delivery Method

To choose how the payment is delivered, follow these steps:

1. Click on Choose Delivery Method: Locate this option during the payment process.

2. Select a Delivery Option:

- **Bank Transfer (ACH Payment):** Send the payment electronically.
- **Check**: Issue a physical check for the payment.

By entering all required details and selecting the appropriate delivery method, you'll maintain accurate records and streamline vendor payments in QuickBooks.

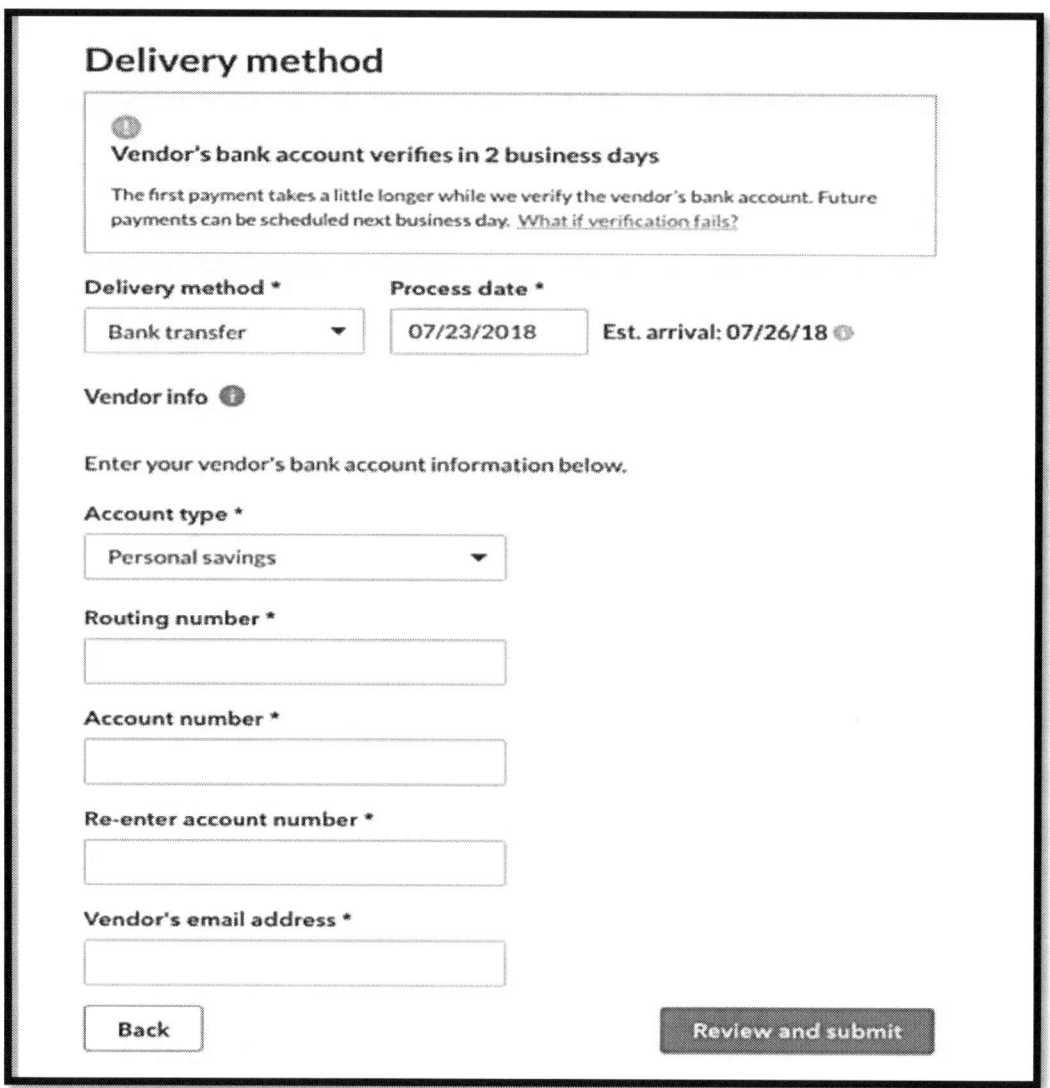

If You Choose to Pay by Check

1. Set the Process Date: Select the date when the payment will be issued.

2. Update Vendor Details (if needed): Ensure vendor information is accurate before proceeding.

Important Notes

Vendor Credits: Always set up vendor credits in advance. These credits can be applied to invoices during payment processing.

Check Numbering: QuickBooks assigns check numbers sequentially to maintain proper internal controls and record accuracy.

By following these steps, you'll ensure smooth and organized vendor payment management using QuickBooks.

SETTING UP ACH BANK TRANSFERS FOR VENDORS

To pay vendors via ACH bank transfer using QuickBooks Online Bill Pay, follow these steps:

1. Add the Vendor's Bank Account:

- Input the vendor's bank details.
- QuickBooks initiates a verification process by sending a small micro-deposit (referred to as a "private bank add") to the vendor's account.

2. Wait for Verification:

- This process usually takes up to two business days to complete.

3. Immediate Payments (If Needed):

- If the vendor needs to be paid immediately, issue a check payment before the bank account verification is complete.
- If the vendor's account is added but not verified, QuickBooks will default to sending a check instead of processing an ACH payment.

4. Post-Verification:

- Once the vendor's account is verified, you can initiate ACH payments starting the next business day.

CREATING VENDOR CREDITS IN QUICKBOOKS ONLINE

Vendor credits help reduce the amount owed to a vendor. Follow these steps to create and apply credits:

1. Create a Vendor Credit:

- Go to the Create (+) menu and select Vendor Credit.
- Enter the vendor's name and fill in the credit details. Ensure all amounts are positive.
- Click Save and Close.

2. Apply the Vendor Credit to an Open Bill:

- Open the bill you want to pay.
- Click Make Payment.
- In the Bill Payment window:
- The open bill will appear under the Outstanding Transactions section.
- Select the vendor credit from the Credits section.
- Click Save and Close.

By setting up ACH payments and managing vendor credits, you can streamline the bill payment process in QuickBooks Online and maintain accurate records with ease.

Scheduling Recurring Bills to Stay Ahead of Deadlines

Recurring transactions in QuickBooks Online help you save time, reduce errors, and streamline repetitive tasks. This feature allows you to:

- Automate recurring journal entries.
- Automatically generate invoices for subscription-based customers.
- Schedule checks or bills to enter automatically.

You can also use recurring transactions to create templates for complex or detailed journal entries and invoices. In QuickBooks Desktop, this functionality is referred to as "Memorizing a Transaction."

What Can You Automate?

QuickBooks Online supports recurring transactions for the following types:

- Bills
- Checks
- Expenses
- Invoices
- Journal Entries
- Purchase Orders
- Sales Receipts

Note: Deposits and bill payments cannot be automated.

Once a recurring transaction is created, you can adjust its type and define how frequently it occurs.

HOW TO CREATE A RECURRING TRANSACTION

1. Access the Settings Menu:

Click the Gear Icon in the QuickBooks toolbar.

2. Under the List column, click Recurring Transactions.

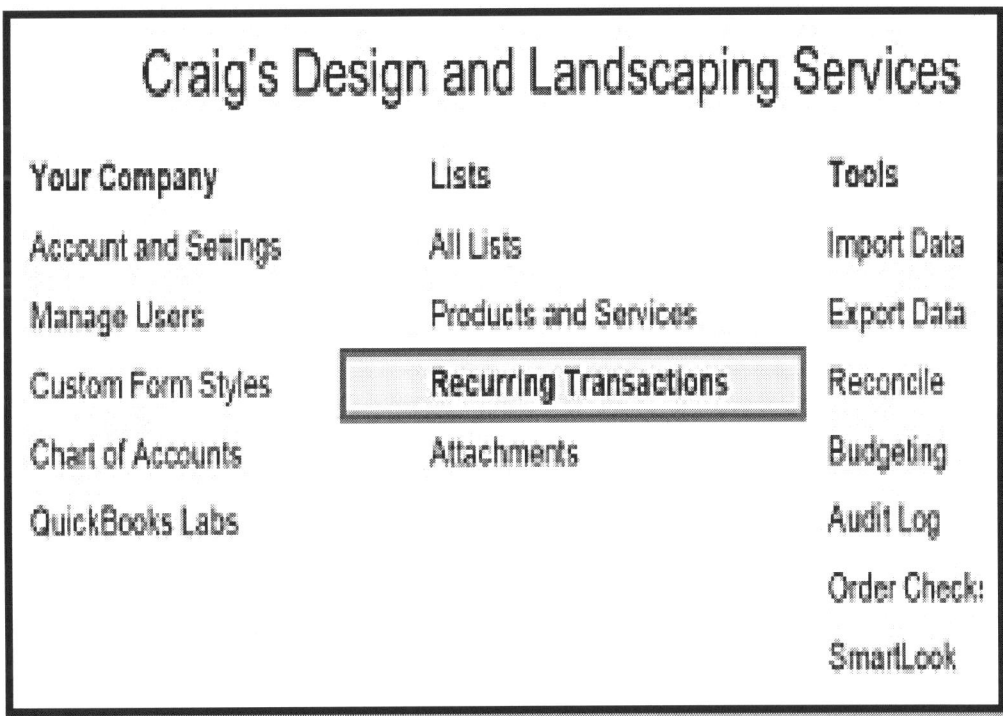

Recurring transactions are an excellent tool for automating routine tasks that occur regularly. They help ensure consistency, save time, and maintain accuracy in your financial records.

Type	Description	Example of Use
Scheduled	This type of recurring transaction creates the selected transaction automatically according to the schedule specified.	Best for transactions that have a fixed amount and fixed schedule, such as: • Customers who are invoiced the same amount each month. • Monthly journal entry to amortize a prepaid asset.
Reminder	This type of recurring transaction reminds the user to create the transaction using the template. Transactions are not generated or saved until the user decides to create them.	Best for transactions with a fixed schedule that need to be edited before they are created, such as: • Utility bills. • Purchase orders for regularly ordered items where the quantity varies.
Unscheduled	This is a template of a transaction that is saved but the transaction is not necessarily complete. This template reduces the need to retype the lines each time it is used.	Best for complicated transactions like a journal entry containing multiple lines with amounts that vary or a frequency that varies, such as: • Payroll journal entry.

3. Begin a New Transaction

- Click New to begin setting up a recurring transaction.

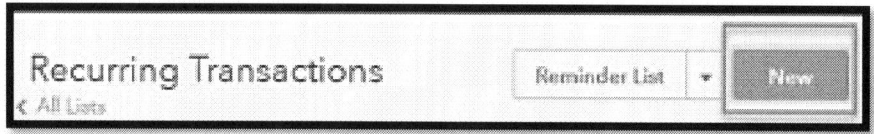

4. choose the Transaction Type

- Choose the Transaction Type of your preference and click OK.

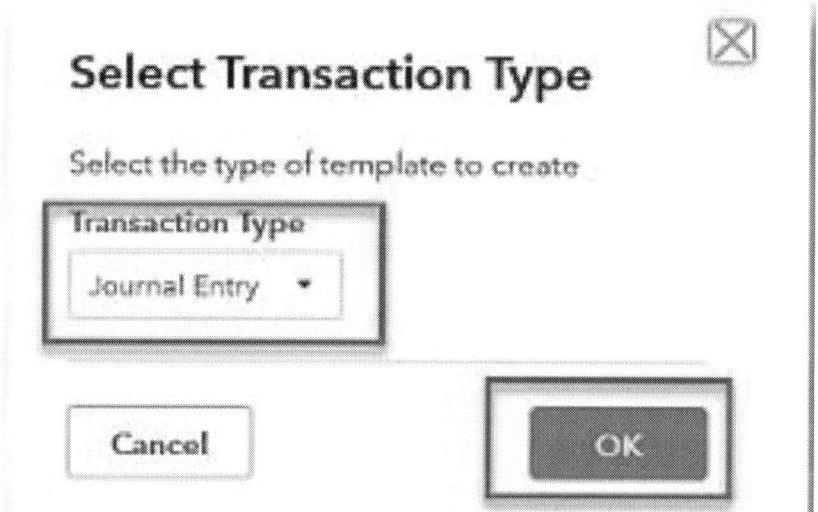

Completing the Details for a Recurring Template

When setting up a recurring transaction in QuickBooks, you'll need to provide specific details to customize the template. Follow these steps:

1. Template Name

Give your template a clear and recognizable name to make it easy to identify later.

2. Transaction Type

Choose one of the three options based on your needs:

- **Scheduled:** Automatically processes the transaction at regular intervals.
- **Reminder**: Sends you a notification to manually process the transaction.
- **Unscheduled:** Saves the transaction for future use without a set schedule.

3. Interval

Define how often the transaction should repeat:

- Daily, Weekly, Monthly, or Yearly.
- Specify the exact day it should occur.

4. Start Date

- Set the start date for the recurring transaction.
- The date must be in the future relative to the template creation date.

5. End Options

Determine how long the recurring transaction will run:

- None: Continues indefinitely.
- Specific End Date: Stops on a particular date.
- Number of Occurrences: Repeats a set number of times.

6. Template Body

- Enter all relevant transaction details, including amounts, accounts, descriptions, and any other required information.

7. Save Template

Once all details are filled in, click Save Template to finalize and activate the recurring transaction.

By completing these steps, you can set up accurate and efficient recurring transactions in QuickBooks, ensuring your records remain up to date and tasks are automated.

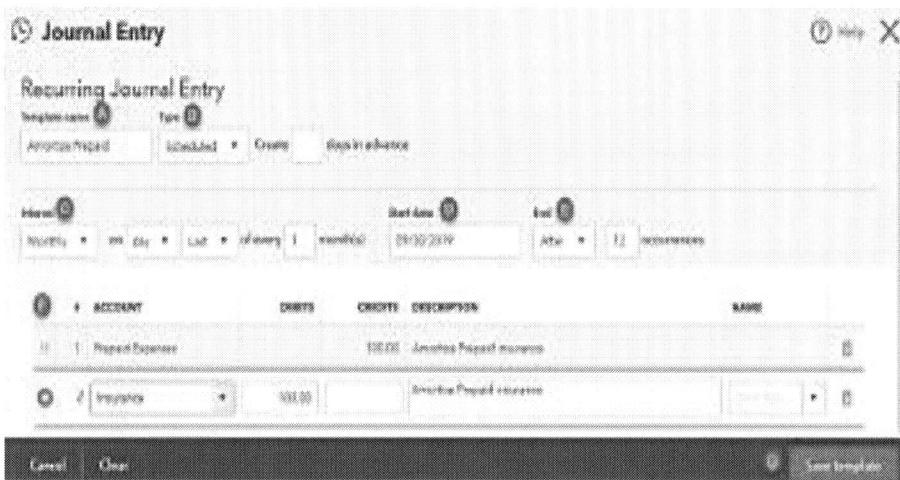

Managing Recurring Transactions

Once you've set up a recurring transaction in QuickBooks, you can easily manage or make changes to it using the Recurring Transactions List. Here's how:

- **Locate the Transaction:** Find the recurring transaction you want to update in the Recurring Transactions List.
- **Edit the Transaction**: Use the Edit option in the Action column on the right-hand side to make any necessary changes.

Tracking Business Expenses for Tax Deductions

Managing recurring transactions not only keeps your finances organized but also simplifies tracking expenses for tax purposes. By maintaining accurate records, you can ensure you capture all eligible deductions and streamline your tax preparation process.

CHAPTER 5

PAYROLL AND EMPLOYEE MANAGEMENT MADE SIMPLE

QuickBooks Payroll Online, created by Intuit, is a cloud-based solution designed to simplify payroll tasks for small and medium-sized businesses. It automates essential processes like salary calculations, tax management, and employee payments, helping businesses streamline their payroll operations with ease.

Integrating Factorial with QuickBooks

Connecting Factorial with QuickBooks allows for seamless employee account setup in QuickBooks Payroll. Once you create an employee profile in Factorial, the system automatically generates a corresponding payroll account in QuickBooks. Here's how to set it up:

1. Install the QuickBooks Integration

Begin by installing the integration tool that connects both platforms.

2. Find Your Company ID

- As an admin, extract your company ID in order to connect QuickBooks to Factorial.

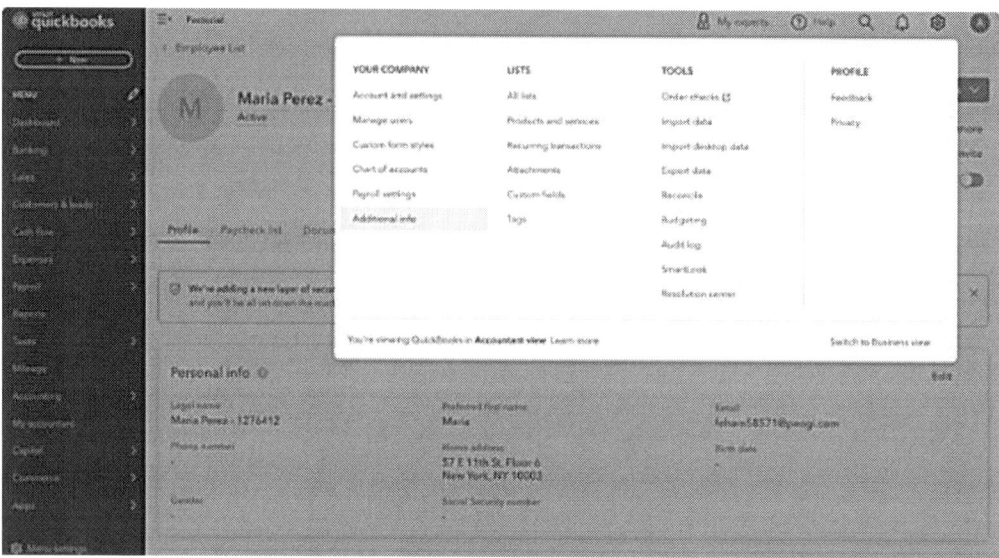

3. Copy the Company ID

- Copy the company ID and use it during the setup process.

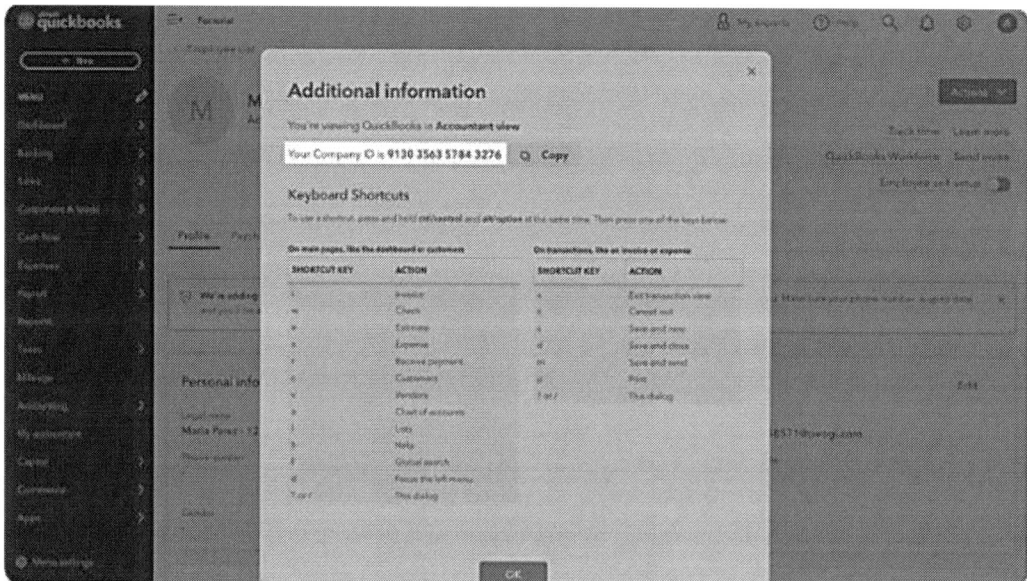

4. Add Employees in Factorial

When a new employee is added in Factorial, the integration automatically creates a payroll account for them in QuickBooks. This automation reduces administrative work and saves time.

5. Ready to Use

Once the integration is set up, it's ready to simplify your processes. You can also explore other Factorial integrations to maximize efficiency.

WHY INTEGRATE PAYROLL AND HR?

Integrating Factorial with QuickBooks Payroll saves time and eliminates repetitive manual tasks. Here's how it benefits your business:

1. Automatic Account Creation

New employees added to Factorial are automatically created in QuickBooks Payroll, removing the need for manual setup.

2. Seamless Onboarding

Streamline the onboarding process by automating payroll account creation, allowing you to focus on other critical tasks.

3. Save Time and Effort

Automation reduces duplicate data entry, saving time and effort while allowing you to prioritize strategic HR initiatives.

4. Consistent Data Management

While not a full synchronization, the integration ensures accurate and consistent data with automated account creation, minimizing manual errors.

5. Smooth Payroll Processing

With employee accounts already in place in QuickBooks, payroll runs seamlessly, ensuring timely and accurate payments.

WHY CHOOSE QUICKBOOKS FOR U.S. PAYROLL?

QuickBooks Payroll Online is a robust tool that automates payroll processes, from salary calculations to tax compliance, helping businesses save time, reduce errors, and stay compliant with regulations.

Key Features of QuickBooks Payroll Online:

1. Payroll Processing

- Automatically calculates wages, bonuses, and payroll taxes.
- Ensures all deductions adhere to legal requirements.

2. Tax Filing

- Prepares and files federal, state, and local tax forms.
- Ensures timely and accurate submissions for compliance.

3. Direct Deposit

- Enables direct payment to employees' bank accounts, eliminating the need for paper checks.

4. Employee Self-Service

- Gives employees access to pay stubs, tax forms, and personal details through a self-service portal.
- Allows employees to update personal information and download year-end tax documents.

5. Integration with QuickBooks Accounting

- Syncs effortlessly with QuickBooks accounting software for streamlined data sharing.
- Simplifies payroll expense tracking and financial reporting.

6. Compliance and Reporting

Provides precise calculations and generates reports to ensure compliance with labor laws.

FLEXIBILITY AND CONVENIENCE

QuickBooks Payroll Online allows business owners to manage payroll from anywhere, anytime, using a web browser. This flexibility ensures payroll operations remain efficient and up to date.

WHY CHOOSE FACTORIAL FOR HR MANAGEMENT?

Factorial is an all-in-one HR management solution designed to simplify processes and seamlessly integrate with payroll tools like QuickBooks. By using Factorial, businesses save time, improve efficiency, and streamline HR and payroll operations. Here's how Factorial can benefit your organization:

1. Simplified HR Management

Centralizes employee data, attendance tracking, time-off requests, and document storage, making HR tasks more organized and efficient.

2. Employee Self-Service Portal

- Empowers employees to manage their HR information independently.
- Enables employees to request time off, access pay stubs, and update personal details, reducing HR's administrative workload.

3. Time and Attendance Tracking

- Provides tools to track work hours, clock-ins/outs, and leave, ensuring payroll accuracy and fair compensation.

4. Streamlined Recruitment and Onboarding

- Simplifies hiring with tools for job postings, application tracking, and automated onboarding tasks, freeing up time for other priorities.

5. Compliance and Document Management

- Stores HR documents securely while tracking expiration dates.
- Generates compliance reports to help ensure adherence to labor regulations.

6. Insights and Analytics

- Offers workforce analytics to uncover trends, identify patterns, and make data-driven decisions for organizational growth.

7. Seamless Integrations

- Connects with payroll systems, calendars, and communication tools to reduce redundant data entry and maintain consistency.

8. Scalable for All Business Sizes

- Adapts to the needs of small, medium, and large businesses, supporting growth at every stage.

The Power of Combining QuickBooks and Factorial

QuickBooks simplifies payroll management, while Factorial streamlines HR processes. Together, they provide a comprehensive solution for workforce management, enabling businesses to:

- Save time with automation.
- Ensure compliance with labor and tax regulations.
- Eliminate complexities through seamless integration.

This combination allows businesses to focus on strategic growth by minimizing administrative burdens and improving accuracy in both payroll and HR management.

AUTOMATING PAYROLL CALCULATIONS AND TAX FILING

Handling payroll manually can be tedious and time-consuming, requiring hours of calculations, spreadsheet management, and check-writing. Unexpected issues, such as employee leave or calculation errors, can further complicate the process. As a business grows, manual payroll systems become inefficient and costly, making payroll automation a practical solution.

What Is Payroll Automation?

Payroll automation uses technology to streamline and simplify payroll tasks, replacing manual processes with efficient, automated systems. Key payroll functions that can be automated include:

- Calculating wages (regular, overtime, and double-time).
- Processing bonuses, commissions, and pay raises.
- Managing deductions and tax calculations.
- Handling retroactive pay, reimbursements, and more.

Most automated payroll systems integrate with enterprise resource planning (ERP) software, giving businesses a comprehensive view of their financial performance.

STEPS TO AUTOMATE PAYROLL

Before automating payroll, ensure all data is accurate and updated. Create a checklist of essential tasks to maintain accuracy. Follow these steps:

1. Use Cloud-Based Time Tracking Software

- Employees can log and submit working hours directly in the software.
- Eliminates manual timesheet calculations and offers real-time access to data.

2. Export Data to Cloud-Based Payroll Software

- Import timesheet data into platforms like QuickBooks Online, which handle tasks such as generating tax forms and calculating payroll taxes.

3. Automate Journal Entries in Accounting Software

- Once payroll is processed, export journal entries directly to accounting software.
- Saves time and ensures accuracy in financial records.

Payroll Tasks You Can Automate

Cloud-based payroll systems simplify a wide range of tasks, including:

- Setting pay schedules.
- Managing benefits deductions.
- Calculating PTO, holidays, and overtime.
- Processing payroll and generating pay stubs or checks.
- Filing and distributing employee tax forms.
- Ensuring compliance with federal, state, and local tax laws.
- Managing worker's compensation and mid-cycle payroll corrections.

BENEFITS OF PAYROLL AUTOMATION

1. Faster Payroll Calculations

Automation eliminates manual calculations, significantly reducing the time spent on payroll tasks while ensuring accuracy.

2. Reduced Human Error

Automated systems minimize errors like incorrect wages or missing data, avoiding costly corrections, employee dissatisfaction, or legal issues.

3. Cost Savings

Reduces the need for a large HR team and lowers operational costs compared to outsourcing payroll services.

4. Simplified Time Tracking

Automatically records and calculates employee hours, relieving HR staff of manual tracking tasks and ensuring accurate pay.

5. Enhanced Security

Payroll systems encrypt and password-protect confidential data, ensuring only authorized personnel can access sensitive information.

6. Easier Tax Calculations

Pre-set tax rates and rules simplify deductions, ensuring compliance with tax laws while reducing administrative burden.

7. Faster Processing

Employees can input their own information into the system, speeding up payroll processing and ensuring timely payments.

8. Improved Record-Keeping

Digitally stores payroll and tax records securely in one place, making it easy to generate reports, analyze data, and streamline tax filings.

Automating payroll transforms a time-intensive process into an efficient, accurate, and secure operation. By reducing human error, saving costs, and enhancing compliance, automation supports businesses in focusing on strategic growth and employee satisfaction.

WHY AUTOMATE PAYROLL?

Automating payroll offers businesses a streamlined process that reduces errors, saves time, and boosts security. With payroll automation, companies can focus on strategic growth while ensuring accurate and timely employee payments. It's a valuable and cost-effective investment, especially for small businesses.

How to Choose an Automated Payroll System

When selecting an automated payroll system, focus on key factors like usability, cost, customer support, integration with other business tools, and scalability for future growth. The system should meet all your payroll needs, including:

- Managing various pay types and commissions.
- Handling diverse employee benefits.

The right system ensures smooth operations and supports your company's unique requirements.

WHY PAYROLL AUTOMATION

Payroll automation is more than a convenience—it's a step toward better business management. Here's why:

- **Improved Cash Flow:** Automating payroll provides better control and forecasting of expenses.
- **Enhanced Data Security**: Sensitive information is encrypted and securely stored.
- **Accurate Financial Insights**: Automation reduces errors, offering a clear and precise financial picture.

By automating payroll, you can focus on the most valuable aspect of your business: your employees. With tools like QuickBooks Online, payroll becomes smooth and error-free. Employees can access a self-service portal to track vacation days, view pay stubs, and download T4/RL1 slips. Year-end tasks are simplified as tax rates are automatically updated, ensuring compliance.

TRACKING EMPLOYEE TIME AND PRODUCTIVITY

The integration of Unrubble with QuickBooks Online makes time tracking more efficient for businesses. This connection allows you to:

- Import Employee Data: Quickly transfer your employee list from QuickBooks to Unrubble without manual entry.
- Export Timesheets: Seamlessly export timesheets from Unrubble to QuickBooks Online by selecting specific periods and employees.

This integration ensures accurate time tracking and record-keeping, enhancing the overall efficiency of payroll management.

How to Connect QuickBooks and Unrubble

By linking these two platforms, businesses can synchronize employee work hours and streamline the payroll process. Stay tuned for step-by-step instructions to connect QuickBooks and Unrubble to simplify your workflow.

Steps to Connect QuickBooks and Unrubble

1. Access Settings in Unrubble

- Log in to your Unrubble account.
- Click on your profile icon and select "Settings" from the dropdown menu.

2. Enable QuickBooks Integration

- Go to the "Integrations" tab on the left sidebar.
- Under the QuickBooks option, click "Connect".

3. Authorize QuickBooks Access

- You'll be redirected to QuickBooks.
- Log in using your QuickBooks credentials and grant permission for Unrubble to access your QuickBooks account.

4. Import Employees from QuickBooks

- Once connected, Unrubble will allow automatic employee imports.
- Navigate to the "Team" section in Unrubble's top menu.
- Click "Import", select "From QuickBooks", choose the employees you want, and click "Import".

5. Export Timesheets to QuickBooks

- In Unrubble, generate the required timesheet report under the "Reports" section.
- Choose the employees and date range.
- Click "Export" and select "To QuickBooks" to transfer the timesheet data.

By integrating QuickBooks with Unrubble, you simplify time tracking and payroll management, saving time and ensuring accuracy.

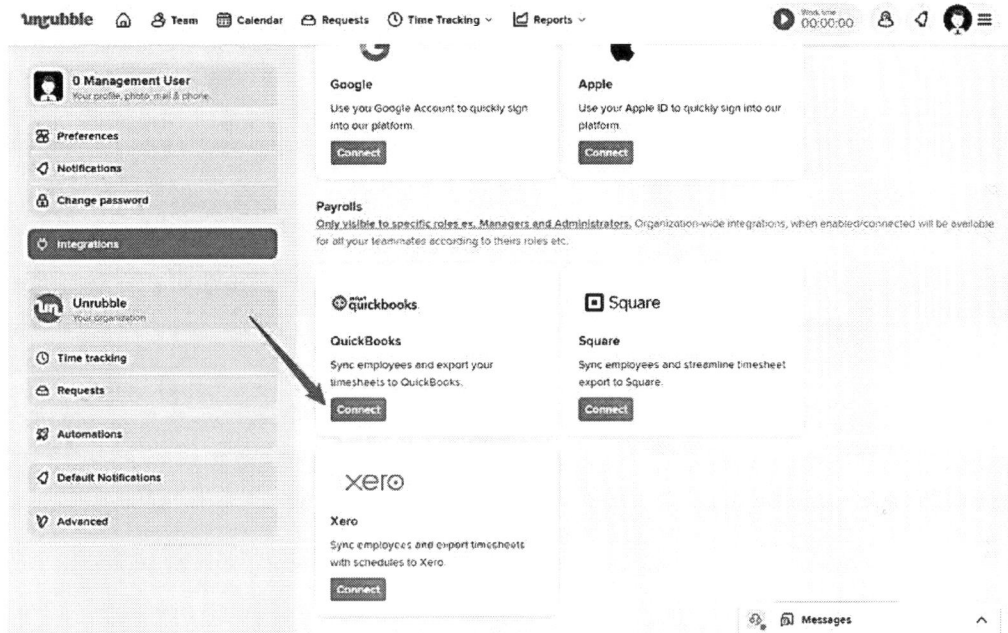

Exporting timesheets to QuickBooks is not available under the "Simple Start" plan. However, for all other plans, integrating Unrubble with QuickBooks ensures seamless data synchronization, improving the accuracy of both employee time tracking and financial management.

Why Integrate QuickBooks Time with Unrubble?

1. Simplified Accounting

Streamline financial tasks, from paying employees to managing bills, by connecting Unrubble with QuickBooks Time.

2. Reduced Errors

Minimize mistakes in recording work hours and financial data, ensuring accurate employee payments.

3. Real-Time Updates

Keep work hours and financial records consistently synchronized to stay on top of your business.

4. Time Savings

Eliminate manual data entry, freeing up time for more strategic tasks.

5. Informed Decision-Making

Leverage accurate and timely data to make smarter decisions about budgeting and team management.

6. Effortless Payroll

Seamlessly transfer work hours to QuickBooks Time for smooth payroll processing and timely employee payments.

7. Labor Law Compliance

Accurately monitor work hours and breaks to ensure compliance with labor regulations.

8. Project Tracking

Track the time spent on projects, helping manage costs and meet deadlines efficiently.

9. Custom Reporting

Generate tailored reports combining financial and work-hour data for a comprehensive view of business performance.

10. Enhanced Transparency

Enable team members to monitor time spent on tasks, fostering trust and accountability.

By integrating QuickBooks Time with Unrubble, your business benefits from simplified time tracking, accurate payroll, and efficient management processes. This integration is a valuable tool for enhancing productivity, compliance, and decision-making across your organization.

MANAGING BENEFITS BONUSES AND CONTRACTOR PAYMENTS

The COVID-19 pandemic spurred a surge in self-employment and small businesses, creating a new wave of entrepreneurs who had to quickly master financial management, including taxes and payments. Today, businesses across industries are leveraging freelancers and gig workers for flexibility while ensuring compliance with IRS regulations.

Hiring independent contractors provides advantages over full-time employees but comes with specific rules and tax obligations. Tools like QuickBooks Online make managing contractor payments and tax reporting more straightforward, but it's essential to set everything up correctly from the start.

Independent Contractor vs. Employee: Understanding the IRS Distinction

Before hiring, ensure your worker is classified correctly as an independent contractor or an employee. The IRS closely monitors worker classification, and misclassifying someone can result in penalties and back taxes.

Independent Contractors: They control how they perform their work and operate independently.

Employees: They follow company oversight regarding their work and how it's completed.

If you're unsure about classification, consult a professional to avoid potential IRS audits or penalties.

Setting Up Contractor Records in QuickBooks Online

Once you've determined that your hire qualifies as an independent contractor, follow these steps to set them up in QuickBooks Online:

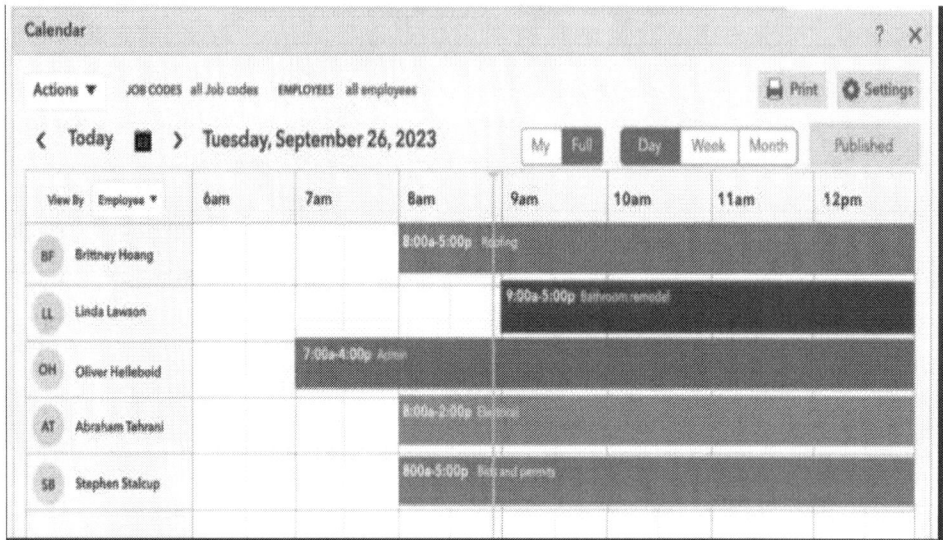

1. Collect Form W-9

Independent contractors must complete IRS Form W-9, providing their taxpayer identification number and verifying their status.

Contractors are responsible for their taxes, filing quarterly estimates, and submitting Form 1040 annually.

2. Add Them as Vendors

In QuickBooks Online, navigate to the Expenses tab, select Vendors, and click New Vendor. Enter the contractor's details and check the box for "Track payments for 1099" to ensure proper tax reporting.

3. Record Payments

- In the Vendor list, locate the contractor's record to track payments.
- If the contractor earns $600 or more in a year, you'll need to generate and file Form 1099-NEC, which QuickBooks can assist with.

- Note: Form 1099-NEC is not required for corporations or LLCs filing as C or S Corporations.

Paying Independent Contractors

QuickBooks Online simplifies contractor payments. Here are the payment options:

1. Bank Transfer (ACH)

Fast, secure, and convenient for processing contractor payments.

2. Check

If you prefer checks, record the payment in the contractor's vendor profile for accurate tax tracking.

3. Credit Card

Pay via credit card for additional benefits, like cash flow management, while recording transactions directly in QuickBooks.

QuickBooks Online automatically tracks these payments, simplifying the process of generating Form 1099-NEC when required.

WHY 1099 COMPLIANCE IS CRUCIAL

The gig economy's growth has drawn increased IRS attention to businesses hiring freelancers. Proper worker classification and accurate filing of 1099 forms are essential to avoid penalties.

- Misclassifying employees as contractors can result in fines.
- Neglecting to file 1099 forms for eligible contractors can lead to costly penalties.

QuickBooks Online helps businesses stay compliant by tracking payments and preparing necessary tax forms.

With the continued rise of self-employment and contract work, setting up contractor records correctly ensures compliance and smooth operations. QuickBooks Online remains a reliable tool for managing contractor payments and meeting tax reporting requirements, helping you build long-term, productive relationships with freelancers while avoiding IRS scrutiny.

CHAPTER 6
REAL TIME FINANCIAL REPORTING

In today's rapidly evolving landscape, staying updated with constant changes is essential for every industry, including accounting. Many businesses are moving away from traditional accounting methods and adopting modern, advanced solutions. One of the most significant advancements is real-time accounting—an innovative approach that provides up-to-the-minute financial reporting and a host of other benefits.

Let's explore the potential of real-time accounting and why it's becoming indispensable in today's business environment.

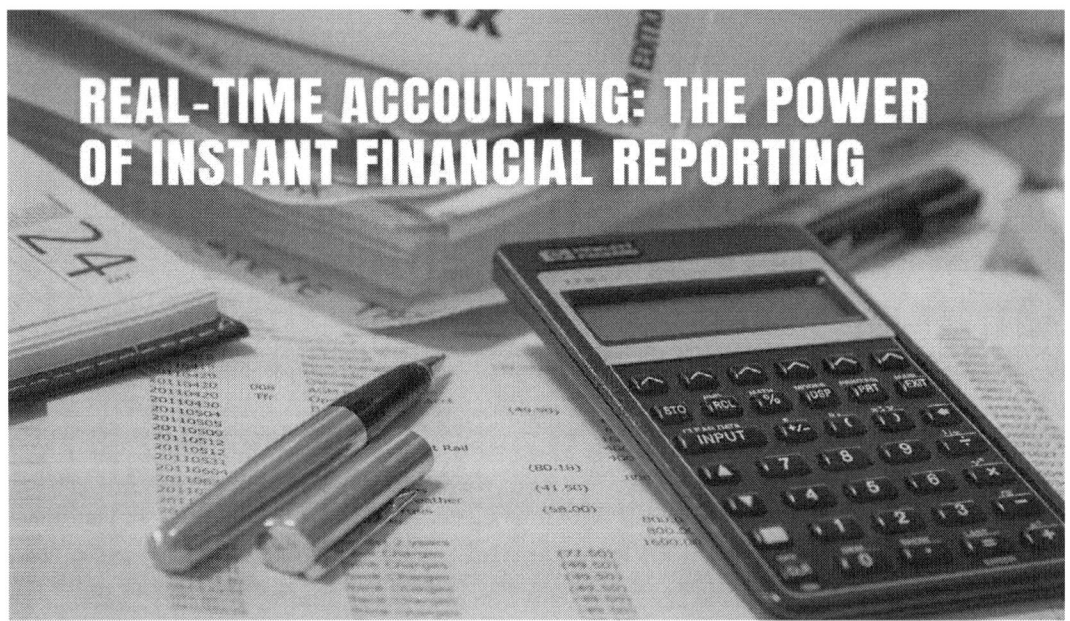

Key Features and Benefits of Real-Time Accounting and Financial Reporting

Real-Time Accounting

Real-time accounting enables businesses to process financial transactions instantly, giving business owners immediate access to updated financial data. This accessibility supports quicker and better-informed decision-making, offering a significant competitive advantage.

Real-Time Financial Reporting

With instant report generation, real-time financial reporting ensures better cash flow management and fosters transparency in financial operations. Businesses can analyze their financial health at any time, supporting more effective planning and execution.

Advantages of Automation

Automation is a cornerstone of real-time accounting. By streamlining financial processes, automation reduces costs, eliminates manual errors, and improves overall efficiency, freeing up valuable time for strategic tasks.

The Role of Cloud Technology

Cloud-based accounting platforms facilitate real-time collaboration and provide secure, remote access to financial data. These systems are equipped with advanced security features to protect sensitive information while allowing seamless integration across teams and locations.

Future Trends in Real-Time Accounting

Emerging trends in this field include the integration of AI and machine learning for advanced data analysis, enhanced analytics for deeper insights, and improved interoperability with other business systems for a more comprehensive operational overview.

Transformative Impact

Real-time accounting empowers businesses to adapt swiftly to market changes, make timely decisions, and maintain a competitive edge. This modern approach to accounting is crucial for ensuring long-term financial success.

THE POWER OF INSTANT FINANCIAL REPORTING

Instant financial reporting, an integral aspect of real-time accounting, allows businesses to generate detailed financial reports on demand. Here's how this capability benefits organizations:

Improved Decision-Making

With financial data readily available, decision-making becomes faster and more informed. The Association for Financial Professionals highlights that real-time data helps businesses respond quickly to market changes, safeguarding their competitive position.

Additionally, investing in financial certifications, like CPA courses, ensures teams are equipped to maximize these advancements.

Better Cash Flow Management

Real-time accounting enables businesses to monitor cash inflows and outflows as they happen, making budgeting and forecasting more accurate. Forbes emphasizes that effective cash flow management is vital, particularly for startups and small businesses, to ensure survival and growth.

Greater Accuracy and Transparency

Traditional accounting often suffers from delays and errors. Real-time updates eliminate these issues, providing accurate data essential for predictive analytics, as noted by Harvard Business Review. Such precision is crucial for effective strategic planning.

AUTOMATION IN REAL-TIME ACCOUNTING

Automation enhances the efficiency of real-time accounting by enabling instant processing of transactions. This offers several key benefits:

- **Cost Reduction**: Automation significantly cuts operational costs by reducing repetitive manual tasks, according to Deloitte's Financial Automation report.
- **Error Minimization:** Research from MIT shows that automation can reduce human errors by up to 90%, ensuring more reliable financial data and better decision-making.
- **Regulatory Compliance:** Automated digital records simplify audits and help businesses meet legal requirements with minimal manual effort, as noted by the Bank for International Settlements.

The Role of Cloud Technology

Cloud technology is a game-changer in real-time accounting due to its scalability, accessibility, and robust security features.

Remote Access

Cloud-based accounting systems allow users to access financial data from anywhere, a feature particularly valuable during disruptions like the COVID-19 pandemic. Forbes highlights how this capability ensures uninterrupted financial operations regardless of location.

Real-time accounting, powered by automation and cloud technology, is shaping the future of financial management. By adopting these innovative solutions, businesses can achieve greater efficiency, accuracy, and adaptability in an ever-changing world.

Real-Time Collaboration

Cloud technology facilitates seamless collaboration by allowing multiple stakeholders to access and update financial records simultaneously. This shared access improves efficiency and ensures everyone is on the same page. According to McKinsey, real-time collaboration significantly boosts productivity and streamlines processes.

High-Level Security

Cloud-based systems offer robust security measures to protect sensitive financial data. With features like encryption, automatic updates, and access controls, these systems provide superior protection compared to traditional on-site solutions. Gartner emphasizes that cloud security is more advanced, reducing the risks associated with data breaches or unauthorized access.

The Future of Real-Time Accounting

The rapid adoption of real-time accounting is shaping the future of finance. Businesses are leveraging automation, enhanced analytics, and cloud integrations to adapt to a fast-paced financial environment.

Artificial Intelligence and Machine Learning

AI and machine learning are revolutionizing real-time accounting. These technologies can process large volumes of data, identify patterns, and deliver actionable insights. As highlighted by the MIT Technology Review, their integration into accounting processes will redefine how financial data is managed and analyzed.

Advanced Analytics Capabilities

Enhanced analytics are becoming a critical component of real-time accounting. According to the Financial Times, advanced insights enable businesses to predict future trends, manage risks effectively, and develop robust growth strategies.

Greater Integration

Real-time accounting is increasingly integrating with other business systems, such as CRM, ERP, and HRM platforms. SAP notes that these integrations provide a unified view of a company's operations, simplifying the management of multiple business functions from a single platform.

Conclusion

As advancements in AI, machine learning, and system integrations continue to evolve, the future of real-time accounting promises more precise and predictive financial tools. These innovations will empower businesses to make smarter decisions, maintain their competitive edge, and navigate the dynamic business landscape with confidence.

UNLOCKING THE POWER OF QUICKBOOKS REPORTS

QuickBooks is a comprehensive accounting software designed to help small businesses streamline their financial management. With robust reporting tools, it enables managers, owners, accountants, and other users to access the critical information they need for efficient business operations. QuickBooks Online enhances this functionality by simplifying report generation and daily tasks, making them faster and more effective.

TYPES OF REPORTS IN QUICKBOOKS

QuickBooks provides a variety of reports tailored to meet diverse business needs:

1. Financial Reports

These offer a detailed overview of a company's financial health:

Income Statement (Profit and Loss Report): Tracks income and expenses over a specific period, providing insights into profitability.

Balance Sheet: Presents a snapshot of the company's financial standing, including assets, liabilities, and equity, at a particular point in time.

2. Inventory Reports

These reports help monitor stock levels, ensuring inventory is managed effectively to meet demand without overstocking.

3. Customer and Vendor Reports

Track transactions and balances with customers and suppliers. These reports are valuable for maintaining strong business relationships and managing accounts effectively.

4. Job Status Reports

Monitor the progress and financial details of ongoing projects. These reports ensure projects stay on schedule and within budget.

WHY USE QUICKBOOKS REPORTS?

QuickBooks reporting empowers users to view, analyze, and interpret their company's financial data, leading to better decision-making and overall business management.

For a deeper understanding of the reports available in QuickBooks Online, Intuit's official guide can provide additional insights and explanations.

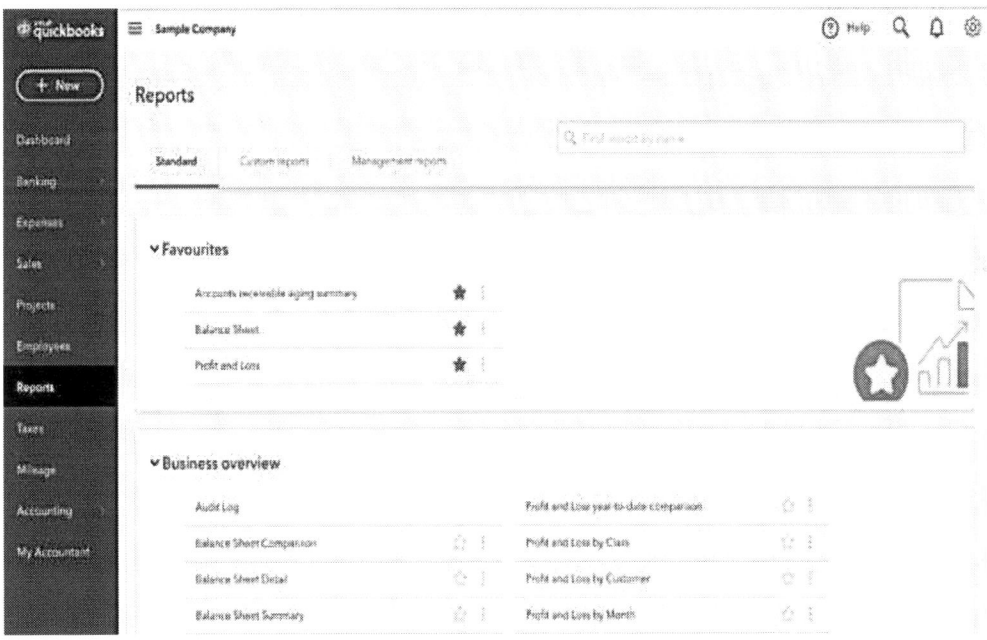

QuickBooks offers various financial reports to help businesses track and analyze their financial activities. Below is a summary of the main types of reports:

Transaction Reports: These reports provide a detailed list of all transactions in QuickBooks, allowing users to check the accuracy and completeness of each entry.

List Reports: Displayed in a structured list format (e.g., charts or graphs), these reports summarize related data for easy reference.

Summary Reports: Offering aggregated data on selected accounts, these reports give a snapshot of financial activities without showing every individual transaction.

Detail Reports: With advanced customization options, these reports track specific transactions across different accounts, providing a deeper look into financial movements.

Inventory Status Reports: Available in QuickBooks Pro and Premier, these reports offer a comprehensive analysis of inventory items, including sales data, to help with inventory **management.**

Job Status Reports: Generated by QuickBooks SalesTracker, these reports track job statuses for customer or user-created jobs, showing due dates and current progress to ensure timely project completion.

Customer Reports: Found in QuickBooks Pro and Premier, these reports cover a broad range of customer-related data. Key report types include:

- Customer Master Lists: Organize customer lists for easy contact management.
- Customer Contact Lists: Track customer details, including contact info and addresses, to enhance communication.
- Customer Balance Sheets: Detail the account balances of individual customers, aiding in credit management and collections.

Vendor Reports: Available in QuickBooks Premier and Pro, these reports help manage vendor relationships. Key report types include:

Vendor Contact Lists: Keep vendor contact information updated for effective communication.

Vendor Balance Sheets: Display outstanding balances with each vendor to help manage accounts payable.

QuickBooks offers a wide range of reporting tools to meet all business needs, from basic to advanced customizations. Its powerful reporting features are accessible online at any time, ensuring businesses can make informed decisions based on the latest financial data.

To explore all the reports available with your QuickBooks Online subscription, visit Intuit's official guide.

QuickBooks Online makes accessing reports simple, with a tabbed interface at the top of the page that allows for quick navigation. One standout feature is Quick Reports, which lets users generate detailed reports with just a few clicks. Located on the Home tab, these reports offer real-time data to keep businesses informed on their financial status.

For users who need advanced customization, QuickBooks offers robust tools that allow for detailed tracking of transactions, creation of cash flow charts, and addressing special reporting needs. Whether you need regular financial analysis or a last-minute report, QuickBooks ensures ease of access and flexibility for comprehensive reporting.

From basic reports to highly tailored solutions, QuickBooks provides the tools necessary for businesses of all sizes to manage financial data efficiently.

If you're considering switching to QuickBooks, the process is smooth with professional assistance. MMCConvert specializes in helping businesses transition to QuickBooks, ensuring a quick and effective setup. Their experts can also assist you in choosing the right version for your business and guide you through the conversion.

Contact MMCConvert today to connect with a QuickBooks conversion expert and unlock the full potential of this powerful accounting software!

CUSTOMIZING REPORTS TO FIT YOUR BUSINESS NEEDS

QuickBooks® Online (QBO) is more than just an accounting tool—it's a robust platform that provides valuable insights into your business's financial health. While it excels at organizing and maintaining accurate records, its true strength lies in its ability to deliver actionable data through its reporting capabilities. Once your financial data is set up in QBO, you can take full advantage of its powerful reporting features.

QBO comes with a variety of standard reports, but its custom reporting tools are where it truly shines. These allow you to tailor reports to focus on what matters most to your business, making it easier to share insights with your team and make data-driven decisions. Below are some examples of how custom reports can benefit your business:

- Track key customer or product activity
- Monitor vendor or payee transactions
- Compare budgeted versus actual spending
- Highlight dollar or percentage variances over time

- Focus on specific general ledger accounts
- Analyze data by department or class

GAIN DEEPER INSIGHTS INTO YOUR FINANCES

Customizable reports in QBO give you the ability to explore your data and uncover meaningful insights. For example, you can create a sales trend report to pinpoint your most profitable products or services and identify areas for improvement. Use custom reports to analyze key customers, vendors, products, sales, and purchase accounts for any time period throughout the year.

You can also track key performance indicators (KPIs) that align with your business goals, ensuring your focus remains on the factors that drive growth. By leveraging QBO's reporting tools, you'll be equipped to make strategic decisions that improve your financial health and set your business on a path toward success.

QBO makes it simple to adjust reports and layouts to meet your specific needs. Instead of exporting data into spreadsheets, you can create a set of custom management reports directly in QBO. Using intuitive drop-down menus and filters, you can refine reports and save them as templates for future use. By naming and saving your custom reports, you'll always have quick access to the exact information you need.

Easily Share Financial Data with Your Team

QBO doesn't just help you create insightful reports—it also simplifies sharing them with others. You can easily share customized reports with your management team, business partners, or advisors using the "Share with" drop-down menu or by emailing the reports. This feature ensures that everyone involved has access to key financial metrics beyond standard Balance Sheets or Profit & Loss statements, fostering better collaboration and informed decision-making.

Clarity for Tax Planning and Beyond

QBO's customizable reporting features give you a clear view of your finances at any time. These reports aren't just useful for day-to-day analysis—they're invaluable for tax planning and year-end preparations. Providing your accountant with organized, detailed reports streamlines the tax process and makes it easier to file accurately and on time. Sharing financial data with your CPA ensures you stay on track and prepared for what's ahead.

With QBO's powerful and flexible reporting tools, you'll have everything you need to tailor reports, gain deeper insights, and share meaningful data—all while keeping your business running smoothly.

USING DASHBOARDS TO MONITOR YOUR FINANCIAL HEALTH

In today's fast-paced business environment, data is essential. For business owners, entrepreneurs, and CEOs, QuickBooks provides dashboards that turn raw financial data into actionable insights. Much like a car dashboard, QuickBooks dashboards give you a real-time view of your business performance, helping you stay in control and make smarter decisions.

What Are QuickBooks Dashboards?

QuickBooks dashboards act as your financial command center. They're the first thing you see when you log in, providing a snapshot of your company's financial health. With customizable widgets and modules, they answer important questions like "Is my business profitable?" or "How do this year's finances compare to last year?"

More than just tracking income and expenses, these dashboards reveal trends and patterns, empowering you to make informed decisions.

KEY FEATURES OF QUICKBOOKS DASHBOARDS

1. Visual Representations of Financial Data

QuickBooks dashboards use graphs, charts, and other visuals to turn complex data into simple, easy-to-understand summaries. Whether you're looking at income comparisons or balance sheets, these visuals allow you to spot trends at a glance.

2. Performance Tracking

Track vital metrics such as cash flow, revenue, and profit and loss summaries. These insights help you monitor progress toward your goals and adjust quickly to changes.

3. Customization Options

Every business is unique, and QuickBooks dashboards reflect that by allowing you to customize the layout. Move, resize, or add widgets to display only the information that matters most to your business.

WHY QUICKBOOKS DASHBOARDS MATTER TO BUSINESS OWNERS

Real-Time Monitoring

QuickBooks dashboards provide real-time updates, alerting you immediately to changes like unexpected expenses or sales spikes. This instant visibility enables quick and effective responses.

Informed Decision-Making

Access to timely, detailed data allows you to analyze past trends, assess current performance, and confidently plan for the future.

Improved Financial Management

By highlighting inefficiencies and offering insight into cash flow, QuickBooks dashboards help you optimize operations and boost profitability.

HOW TO MAKE THE MOST OF QUICKBOOKS DASHBOARDS

Set Goals and Track Key Metrics

Align your dashboards with your business objectives by setting clear KPIs. This ensures you're focused on tracking progress toward the goals that matter most.

Consistent Monitoring and Analysis

Regularly review your dashboards to stay informed about your financial health. Consistent monitoring helps you respond promptly to changes, while frequent analysis reveals trends, opportunities, and areas needing attention.

Turning Insights Into Action

The real power of dashboards lies in how you use them. Leverage the data to create strategies, perform forecasts, and make proactive decisions. By staying ahead of challenges and seizing opportunities, your business can thrive.

A Trusted Partner for Your Business

QuickBooks dashboards are more than financial tools—they're your trusted ally in managing your company's financial journey. In today's world, where adaptability and quick decision-making are critical, these dashboards equip you to lead with confidence.

By embracing the power of QuickBooks dashboards, you adopt a smarter, data-driven approach to managing your business. These dashboards aren't just features—they're a gateway to growth, a foundation for informed leadership, and a cornerstone of your company's financial success. Take control of your business's future by unlocking the insights hidden within your data.

SPOTTING TRENDS AND OPPORTUNITIES FOR GROWTH

QuickBooks, developed by Intuit, is the world's leading accounting software for small and medium-sized businesses. It simplifies financial management by helping users track income, manage expenses, automate accounting tasks, and create detailed financial reports. Designed with simplicity in mind, QuickBooks is ideal for entrepreneurs and professionals looking for an efficient, user-friendly alternative to traditional accounting systems.

Who Is QuickBooks For?

QuickBooks is tailored to meet the needs of small and medium-sized businesses (SMBs), freelancers, entrepreneurs, and self-employed individuals—especially those without a dedicated accounting team. Its versatility makes it a valuable tool across industries such as:

- Retail
- Hospitality
- Healthcare
- Professional services
- Construction

Many accounting professionals, bookkeepers, and financial advisors also rely on QuickBooks to streamline their workflows and often recommend it to their clients.

Custom Solutions for Diverse Needs

QuickBooks offers various versions to meet specific business requirements:

- QuickBooks Online for flexibility and remote access.
- QuickBooks Desktop for those who prefer locally installed software.
- QuickBooks Self-Employed for freelancers and gig workers.

This adaptability ensures that businesses of all sizes and models can find a solution that fits their needs.

Marketing Approach

QuickBooks' marketing strategy focuses on accessibility and ease of use. The brand leverages digital advertising through search engines and social media to raise awareness and connect with a broad audience, emphasizing its suitability for businesses looking for simplicity and efficiency.

QuickBooks is more than just accounting software—it's a growth enabler, empowering businesses to spot trends, identify opportunities, and make smarter financial decisions with ease.

MARKETING STRATEGIES THAT DRIVE QUICKBOOKS' SUCCESS

QuickBooks employs four key strategies to create value: content, partnerships, customer support, and innovation. These approaches are designed to simplify financial management while building trust, expanding reach, and fostering customer loyalty.

Content Marketing

QuickBooks uses a comprehensive content strategy that includes blog posts, eBooks, video tutorials, and webinars. These resources make accounting concepts easier to understand and highlight the software's practical applications. By acting as a trusted financial advisor, QuickBooks builds credibility and strengthens trust with its audience.

Strategic Partnerships

Collaborating with accountants, bookkeepers, and financial institutions allows QuickBooks to expand its reach. Referral programs and incentives encourage these professionals to recommend the software, leveraging their expertise to attract new users.

Customer Support and Training

Customer satisfaction is a top priority. QuickBooks provides:

- Live chat and helplines for immediate assistance.
- Online guides and training modules to help users quickly adapt to the software.

These efforts reduce the learning curve and foster long-term loyalty.

Innovation and Data-Driven Insights

QuickBooks stays ahead of the competition by:

- Using AI-powered automation and third-party integrations to enhance its features.
- Gathering insights from user behavior, market trends, and competitor analysis to refine its strategies.

Customer feedback and success stories are also used in user-generated content campaigns, driving trust and engagement.

Building Authority and Engagement

QuickBooks positions itself as a financial advisor through resources like whitepapers, case studies, and webinars. These tools help businesses overcome challenges and identify opportunities, strengthening QuickBooks' authority in the financial space.

Further engagement is driven through:

- Personalization using data analytics to address industry-specific challenges.
- Marketing automation to deliver content tailored to prospects' stages in their journey.
- Social media activities, including live Q&A sessions, community interactions, and user-generated content to create a sense of community among users.

A Holistic Approach

QuickBooks has moved beyond product promotion to embrace community involvement, social responsibility, and diversity, equity, and inclusion initiatives. These efforts enhance its brand reputation, foster loyalty, and contribute to sustainable growth.

Despite evolving strategies, QuickBooks' core mission remains unchanged: empowering businesses and supporting their financial success.

CHAPTER 7
TAX SEASON SIMPLIFIED

As 2024 wraps up, accountants and business owners alike will start preparing financial records for the new year. QuickBooks Online (QBO) offers a variety of features to simplify year-end tasks and ensure a smooth start to 2025. Below are key tools and best practices to optimize your year-end preparation:

1. Expense Management with Auto-Categorization

QuickBooks' enhanced auto-categorization feature automatically assigns transactions to predefined categories, saving time and reducing errors.

How to Use:

- Set up or update transaction categories under Banking > Rules based on vendors or keywords.
- Review categorized transactions in Banking > Categorize to verify accuracy and resolve discrepancies before filing taxes.

2. Bank and Credit Card Reconciliation

QBO's updated reconciliation tools make it easier to match transactions with bank statements, ensuring accurate records.

Steps for Reconciliation:

- Navigate to Accounting > Reconcile, select the account, and enter the ending balance from the latest statement.
- Filter for unreconciled transactions and ensure the Difference column equals zero to balance your records.

3. Year-End Reports

QuickBooks offers customizable reports to provide a clear view of client finances.

Key Reports to Run:

- Profit & Loss Report: Access via Reports > Profit & Loss to compare income and expenses.
- Balance Sheet Report: Find it under Reports > Balance Sheet for an overview of assets and liabilities.

- Trial Balance Report: Go to Reports > Accountant Reports for a summary of debits and credits.

Use filters like class or location to tailor reports for specific insights.

4. 1099 Tracking and E-Filing

QBO simplifies contractor payment tracking and streamlines 1099-NEC and 1099-MISC preparation.

How to Set Up:

- In Expenses > Vendors, enable Track payments for 1099 for applicable contractors.
- Double-check vendor classifications and W-9 information under Expenses > Vendors > Prepare 1099s.

5. Accounts Receivable and Invoice Management

QuickBooks' batch invoicing tools streamline the review of accounts receivable (A/R).

Steps for A/R Review:

- Run the Open Invoices Report via Sales > Invoices to track outstanding payments.
- In Sales > Customers, select open items for batch customer payments and apply them to respective invoices.
- Access the A/R Aging Report under Reports > Accountant Reports to identify aged accounts and write them off if necessary.

6. Cash Flow Projections for 2025

QBO's cash flow projection tool provides forward-looking insights to help clients budget for the new year.

How to Use:

- Go to Dashboard > Business Overview > Cash Flow, and create projections using average income and expenses.
- Add any anticipated changes for a comprehensive forecast.
- Review the summary to help clients allocate funds effectively for Q1 2025.

Streamline Your Year-End Tasks with QuickBooks Online

With tools like these, QuickBooks Online simplifies year-end processes, ensuring you head into 2025 with accurate and organized records. Let us know how we can assist in making your year-end process seamless!

PREPARING FOR TAX TIME WITH QUICKBOOKS ONLINE

Tax season is often the busiest time for accountants, filled with tasks like coordinating with clients, cleaning up financial data, and conducting thorough reviews. Before you take a well-earned holiday break, it's worth considering how to set up your practice for a smooth tax-filing season. By leveraging automation and integrating the right tools, you can improve efficiency and minimize stress. One such solution is the Prep for Taxes integration between QuickBooks Online Accountant and Intuit ProConnect Tax, designed to simplify and speed up the tax preparation process by consolidating key activities into one platform.

What Is Prep for Taxes?

Prep for Taxes is a seamless integration that consolidates essential financial data—such as profit and loss statements—onto a single platform. It allows you to make adjustments easily, with any changes automatically syncing from QuickBooks Online Accountant to ProConnect Tax. This eliminates the need for switching between systems, saving time and enhancing accuracy.

Key Features to Optimize Tax Preparation

1. Tax-Ready Balance Sheet

Prep for Taxes generates a tax-ready balance sheet that simplifies reconciliation and ensures accurate data. It aligns financial records with tax returns, reducing errors and making the filing process smoother.

> CPA Insight: "Using ProConnect Tax with QuickBooks Online Accountant saves time, eliminates manual work, and avoids keying errors," says Lisa Brann.

2. Automatic Mapping to Tax Forms

Accounts are automatically mapped to the correct lines on tax forms in ProConnect Tax, saving time and minimizing errors. This feature can save up to 38 minutes per tax return, making it a game-changer for meeting tight deadlines.

3. Real-Time Adjustments Without Data Disruption

Make real-time tax-specific adjustments within ProConnect Tax without altering original bookkeeping data in QuickBooks Online. This ensures that accounting records remain intact while tax-specific changes are handled efficiently.

4. Centralized Tax Data

With Prep for Taxes, all tax-related data is centralized, making it easy to access and share across your team. This streamlined approach enhances collaboration, keeps everyone aligned, and boosts productivity during tax season.

5. Snapshot of Income and Expenses

The tool provides an up-to-date snapshot of client income and expenses, ensuring you're always on track with tax deadlines. This real-time view supports proactive planning and ensures all critical information is ready for filing.

6. Better Organization and Categorization

Prep for Taxes helps accurately categorize transactions, minimizing errors and saving time during reconciliation. This level of organization ensures a smoother filing process and reduces the risk of costly mistakes.

7. Improved Client Communication

Easily share financial data with clients and address their concerns promptly. This streamlined communication fosters better collaboration and strengthens client relationships, making tax preparation a more efficient and positive experience.

8. Efficient Review and Editing

Review and edit client transactions with ease. Quick adjustments ensure data accuracy and compliance, reducing the risk of errors and preparing you for smoother audits if necessary.

SIMPLIFY TAX SEASON WITH PREP FOR TAXES

By combining automation, centralized data, and seamless integration, Prep for Taxes helps accountants work smarter, not harder. With features that enhance accuracy, improve collaboration, and save time, you can navigate tax season with confidence and set your practice up for success.

Preparing for Success in Tax Season

Tax season doesn't have to be overwhelming. With tools like Prep for Taxes, you can automate repetitive tasks, minimize manual data entry, and improve accuracy. These innovations can help you provide exceptional service to your clients while making the season less stressful for you. Don't wait—start integrating these time-saving tools now to ensure a productive and successful January!

Embracing the Prep for Taxes feature can turn tax season into a time of efficiency and opportunity. This platform simplifies the tax preparation process by consolidating essential tools and cutting down on the traditional workload, such as data review and return finalization. With all functionalities in one place, you can save time and focus on more strategic areas of your practice, like strengthening client relationships and expanding your business.

These advanced features are designed to streamline workflows, minimize errors, and help you deliver exceptional service that builds client loyalty. Not only does this simplify tax preparation, but it also lays the groundwork for a stronger and more sustainable practice.

Generating Tax Reports to Hand Off to Your Accountant

If you need a summary of taxable and non-taxable sales along with the total sales tax collected, you can run the Sales Tax Liability Report in QuickBooks Online by following these steps:

1. Access Reports

Navigate to the Reports section.

2. Locate the Report

In the search bar labeled "Find report by name," type Sales Tax Liability report and select it from the results.

3. Set the Report Period

Use the drop-down menu under Report period to select the appropriate date range based on your tax filing frequency.

4. Select Tax Agency

Under Tax Agency, choose a specific agency or select All to include all tax agencies.

5. Run the Report

Click Run report to generate the report.

In the report, the Tax Amount column displays the total sales tax collected for both state and local (city, county, district) taxes.

For more detailed information, click on any amount in the Tax Amount column. This opens a transaction report showing details of individual sales, including the tax charged, customer information, transaction date, and tax rate applied.

ADJUSTING TAX AMOUNTS

If you need to adjust the amount owed due to tax credits, discounts, or corrections, QuickBooks Online provides the option to add tax adjustments. For detailed instructions on making these adjustments, refer to QuickBooks' official support resources.

Filing Sales Tax Returns and Recording Payments

To file your sales tax return and record payments:

1. Go to Taxes

Click on the Taxes tab and select Sales tax.

2. Review Returns

Locate the return you've filed and click Review sales tax.

3. Record Payment

Choose the filing method and click Record payment.

4. Add Payment Information

Enter the tax amount, payment date, bank account, and other necessary details.

5. Record

Click Record payment to finalize the process.

AVOIDING COMMON TAX FILING MISTAKES

Filing taxes can be challenging, especially with constantly changing regulations, but errors can lead to overpaying or delays. By following these streamlined processes and utilizing tools like Prep for Taxes, you can avoid common mistakes, save time, and ensure compliance. Make this tax season an opportunity for accuracy, efficiency, and success.

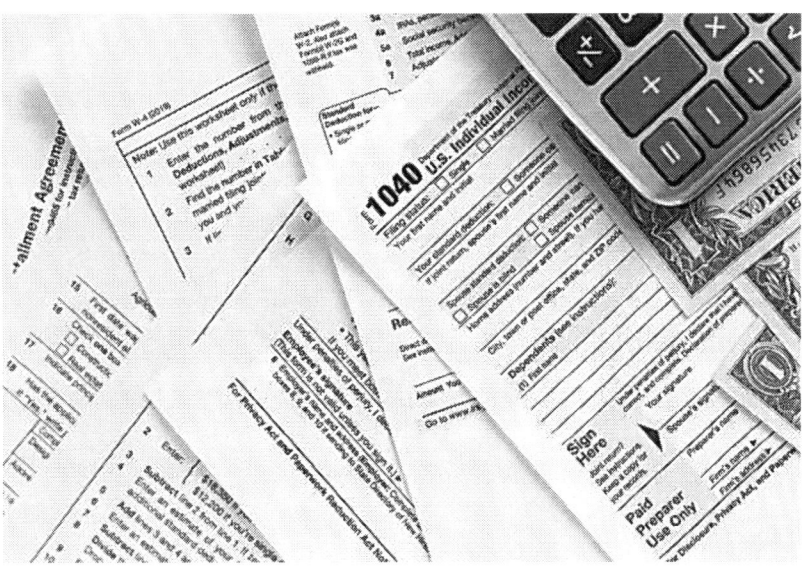

Navigating Tax Changes and Avoiding Filing Mistakes

The 2025 tax season introduces updates in tax brackets, credits, and new Beneficial Ownership Information (BOI) requirements, creating challenges for both individuals and corporations. Below are common mistakes and practical tips to help maintain compliance and avoid costly errors.

Mistake 1: Misreporting Income

A frequent error is failing to report all income, particularly with the rise of the gig economy and alternative income sources like interest earnings or cryptocurrency transactions. The IRS has increased its focus on digital asset reporting, making accurate documentation essential.

KEY UPDATES FOR 2025 TAX RETURNS:

Standard Deduction Increase:

- Single filers: $15,000 (up from $14,600 in 2024).
- Married couples filing jointly: $30,000 (up from $29,200 in 2024).

Tax Brackets Adjusted:

- The 24% tax bracket starts at $103,350 for single filers (up from $95,376 in 2024).
- Foreign Earned Income Exclusion: Increased to $130,000 (up from $126,500).

Corporate Tax Challenges

For corporations, stricter IRS rules now govern the documentation of foreign and digital income. Inadequate reporting of digital assets or overseas transactions can lead to severe penalties. Businesses must carefully document all income sources to ensure compliance and minimize unnecessary payments.

CHOOSING THE WRONG FILING STATUS

Selecting the correct filing status is vital for determining tax rates and deductions.

For Individuals:

Choosing the wrong status, such as Single instead of Head of Household, can lead to missed deductions or credits. For example, the standard deduction for Heads of Household is $22,500 in 2025, compared to $15,000 for Single filers.

For Businesses:

Ensure the entity structure aligns with tax strategy. For instance, an LLC taxed as a sole proprietorship may face higher self-employment taxes and miss out on benefits like the Qualified Business Income (QBI) deduction.

OVERLOOKED DEDUCTIONS AND CREDITS

Failing to claim available deductions and credits can cost individuals and businesses significantly.

Individual Deductions:

- Student Loan Interest: Deduct up to $2,500 (subject to income limits).
- Home Office Expenses: Qualify if part of your home is used exclusively for work.
- Unreimbursed Medical Expenses: Deduct expenses exceeding 7.5% of adjusted gross income, including treatments and prescriptions.

Key Business Credits:

- **R&D Tax Credit**: Rewards innovation but requires proper documentation.
- **Employee Retention Credit (ERC):** Available for businesses retaining employees during COVID-19-related hardships (March 12, 2020– January 1, 2022). Businesses can retroactively claim this credit for prior years until April 15, 2025.

Tax Information Errors

Providing inaccurate or incomplete information is another common issue.

For Individuals:

- Using the wrong Social Security number.
- Address mismatches.
- Claiming deductions or credits you don't qualify for.

For Businesses:

- Tax ID number discrepancies.
- Mismatched filing statuses.
- Missing or incomplete financial statements.

By staying informed about tax updates, choosing the correct filing status, and accurately reporting income, both individuals and businesses can avoid common mistakes. Leveraging the available deductions, credits, and tax planning strategies will ensure compliance and optimize your financial outcomes this tax season.

Late Payment Penalties

Missing tax filing deadlines is one of the easiest mistakes to avoid, yet it happens more often than you might expect.

For Individuals:

- Late Filing Penalty: A 5% penalty is charged on unpaid taxes for each month (or part of a month) that your return is late, capped at 25% of the total balance.
- Late Payment Penalty: A 0.5% penalty is applied each month to unpaid taxes, also capped at 25%.

For Businesses:

- Quarterly Estimated Taxes: Missing quarterly tax deadlines can result in underpayment penalties, especially if your income varies significantly throughout the year.
- Tax Credit Deadlines: Filing late for credits like the R&D Tax Credit may cause you to miss valuable opportunities.
- Annual Returns and Extensions: Failing to file annual returns or request extensions on time can lead to additional penalties and complications.

By understanding these common tax filing errors and planning ahead, you can avoid penalties, reduce stress, and maintain a good standing with the IRS.

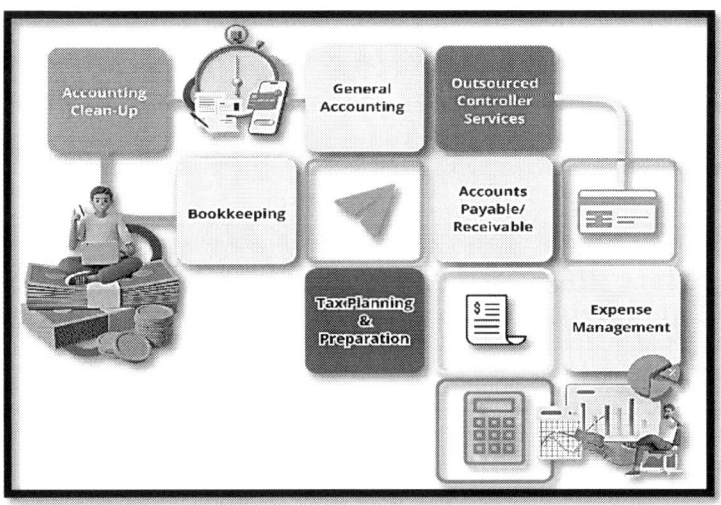

MISUNDERSTANDING STATE AND LOCAL TAX RESPONSIBILITIES

Managing taxes becomes more complex when your business operates in multiple states or if you frequently travel for work. Each state has unique income tax rates, residency rules, and healthcare mandates. For businesses, state-specific sales and income tax regulations vary widely. Understanding your obligations in every state where you operate is essential to avoid noncompliance or the risk of double taxation.

Outdated Records

Keeping your personal and business information up-to-date with the IRS is crucial to avoiding various complications, including:

- **Delayed Refunds:** Personal information mismatches—like a name change after marriage or divorce—can lead to refund delays.
- **Missed Tax Benefits**: Failing to update dependent status may result in lost credits or deductions for individuals. Similarly, businesses may miss out on valuable tax credits if their records are outdated.
- **Noncompliance Penalties:** Incorrect or outdated information can lead to penalties, audits, or other costly consequences for both individuals and businesses.

At Fusion, our CPAs are experts in ensuring tax compliance. From identifying overlooked deductions to managing multi-state tax complexities, we're here to simplify the process and make tax filing seamless for you.

CHAPTER 8
ADVANCED FEATURES FOR GROWING BUSINESSES

Did you know that 88% of all spreadsheets contain errors, with 50% of those used by large companies having critical issues? For HVAC businesses operating on tight margins, this highlights the risks of relying on manual financial processes. Automated solutions like QuickBooks can offer a reliable alternative, simplifying financial management so you can focus on what matters most: delivering exceptional customer service.

How QuickBooks Can Transform Your HVAC Business

QuickBooks brings a wealth of tools to streamline your operations. In this guide, we'll dive into its key features, practical steps to get started, and how integrating QuickBooks with HVAC service software can enhance your workflows. Plus, you'll get a step-by-step guide on maximizing its potential.

Why QuickBooks is Perfect for HVAC Businesses

HVAC companies face unique financial hurdles, from managing labor and material costs to handling payroll, invoicing, and tax preparation. These tasks can be time-consuming and prone to errors, but QuickBooks provides an automated solution to make them manageable.

Here's how QuickBooks simplifies financial management:

- **Time-Saving Automation:** Automate tasks like payroll and recurring invoices to reclaim valuable time each week.
- **Better Cash Flow Visibility:** Monitor expenses in real-time and generate custom reports for a clear financial overview.
- **Improved Accuracy**: Minimize costly errors by keeping financial data well-organized and tax-compliant.

Whether you're a small HVAC business looking to expand or an established company refining your processes, QuickBooks equips you with the tools to manage your finances efficiently and precisely.

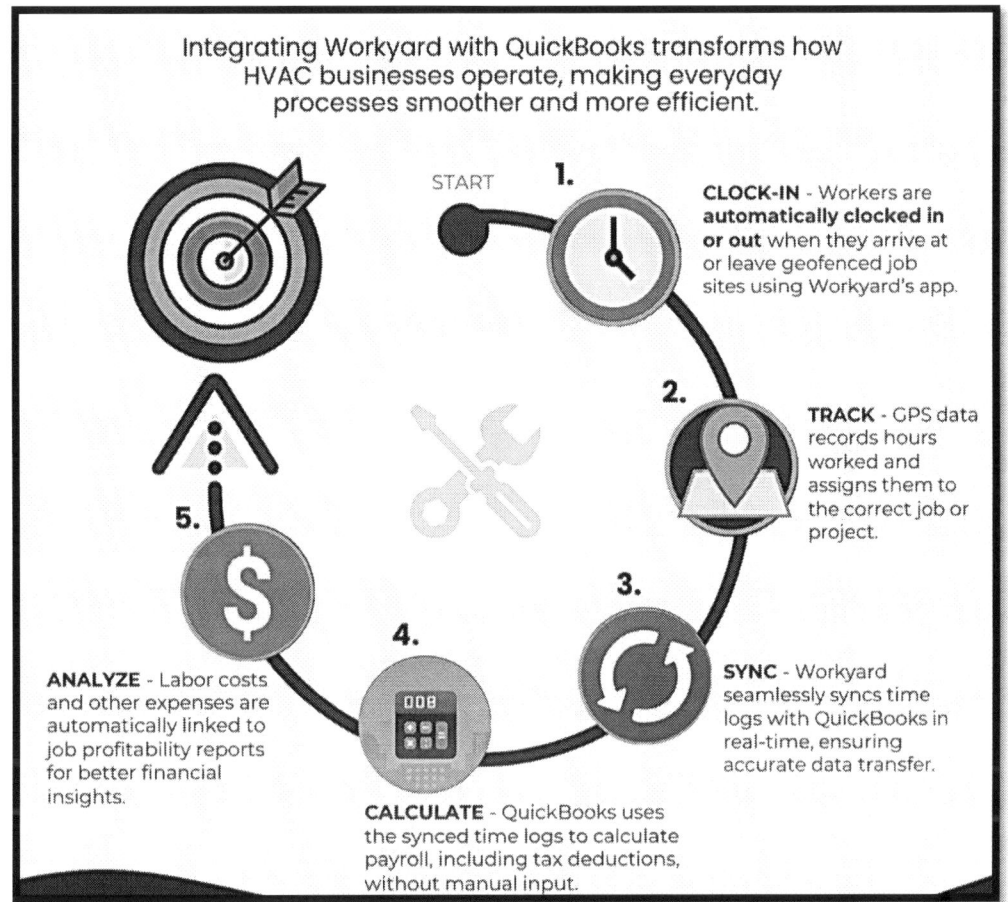

Integrating Workyard with QuickBooks transforms how HVAC businesses operate, making everyday processes smoother and more efficient.

START

1. CLOCK-IN - Workers are **automatically clocked in or out** when they arrive at or leave geofenced job sites using Workyard's app.

2. TRACK - GPS data records hours worked and assigns them to the correct job or project.

3. SYNC - Workyard seamlessly syncs time logs with QuickBooks in real-time, ensuring accurate data transfer.

4. CALCULATE - QuickBooks uses the synced time logs to calculate payroll, including tax deductions, without manual input.

5. ANALYZE - Labor costs and other expenses are automatically linked to job profitability reports for better financial insights.

HOW WORKYARD CAN ELEVATE YOUR HVAC BUSINESS

1. Precise Time Tracking

Workyard takes time tracking beyond QuickBooks' basic capabilities. It uses automated clock-ins when employees enter a geofenced job site and trims clock-out times to their last location, ensuring accurate tracking.

2. Reduce Payroll Waste

Eliminating errors from inaccurate time entries helps HVAC businesses save thousands of dollars annually on payroll expenses.

3. Seamless QuickBooks Integration

Workyard seamlessly syncs employee hours with QuickBooks, eliminating the need for manual data entry and saving valuable time.

4. Improved Job Costing

Assign employee hours directly to specific jobs, providing a clear picture of labor costs and enhancing your ability to track job profitability.

QUICKBOOKS FEATURES BUILT FOR HVAC BUSINESSES

QuickBooks isn't just a standard accounting solution—it's designed to meet the unique needs of HVAC professionals.

1. Streamlined Invoicing

Ditch paper templates and basic tools. QuickBooks lets you create professional, branded invoices with your logo, itemized charges for labor, parts, and equipment, and send them directly to customers via email. It also tracks paid and overdue invoices, so you never miss a follow-up.

2. Job Cost Tracking

Monitor expenses such as materials, labor, and subcontractors at current market prices for every project. Analyze profitability at any stage, especially for long-term projects, and ensure you stay within budget.

3. Simplified Payroll

QuickBooks automates tax calculations, compliance checks, and employee payments, streamlining payroll management. It's perfect for handling salaried employees, hourly workers, and subcontractors, saving time and reducing errors.

4. Inventory Management

Real-time inventory tracking keeps your operations running smoothly. QuickBooks alerts you when supplies need reordering and links inventory data to job costs, ensuring every expense is accounted for.

5. Custom Reports

Generate detailed reports tailored to your business needs, such as cash flow analysis, expense tracking, and job profitability insights. These reports empower you to make informed decisions and improve operations.

Why QuickBooks is a Smart Choice for HVAC Businesses

QuickBooks is more than an accounting tool—it's a strategic partner that helps HVAC businesses operate efficiently. By automating financial tasks and providing actionable insights, it frees you to focus on growing your business and delivering top-notch service.

Choosing the Right QuickBooks Version for Your HVAC Business

Deciding between QuickBooks Online and QuickBooks Desktop is the first step to organizing and automating your financial management. Both options are robust, but the ideal choice will depend on your business size, team structure, and workflow preferences.

INVENTORY MANAGEMENT AND TRACKING MADE SIMPLE

Managing inventory can feel like a delicate balancing act, especially during peak seasons when stockouts and overstocking can cause significant headaches. While there's no magic wand to solve these challenges, implementing a reliable inventory tracking system can work wonders. With real-time insights into your stock, such a system can boost profits, enhance customer satisfaction, and streamline operations.

Today's market offers a wide range of inventory software, from integrated platforms to standalone solutions. Choosing the best fit depends on your business's unique needs and budget. Let's explore how QuickBooks inventory management can simplify your processes, its benefits, and some considerations to keep in mind.

Benefits of Inventory Tracking with QuickBooks Online

An inventory tracking system is a game-changer for businesses that deal with physical goods. It empowers you to make timely, informed decisions, helping you adapt to market fluctuations while avoiding stock shortages or overstocking. Here are the key advantages of using QuickBooks Online for inventory management:

1. Enhanced Customer Satisfaction

Accurate stock tracking ensures you can meet customer demands without running into stockouts. Avoiding these situations prevents lost sales, keeps customers happy, and protects your brand's reputation.

2. Cost Savings on Storage and Waste

While overstocking might seem like a safe option, it increases storage costs and risks spoilage or obsolescence. An efficient tracking system helps you maintain the right balance, stocking only what's needed and saving money and space.

3. Streamlined Operations

QuickBooks allows you to track inventory location and status (e.g., damaged or reserved), speeding up order fulfillment and warehouse workflows. This operational efficiency reduces labor costs and saves valuable time.

4. Better Decision-Making

With accurate inventory data, you can analyze demand patterns, sales trends, and seasonal fluctuations. These insights enable smarter decisions about pricing, promotions, purchasing, and production planning, giving your business a competitive edge.

5. Reduced Shrinkage and Theft

Inventory tracking helps identify discrepancies between actual stock and recorded data, highlighting potential losses due to shrinkage or theft. This added layer of control safeguards your assets and improves accountability.

6. Improved Supplier Relationships

Accurate inventory forecasting fosters better communication with suppliers. By minimizing last-minute orders or cancellations, you build trust and strengthen long-term partnerships.

Choosing the Right Inventory Tracking Solution

To enjoy these benefits, it's essential to select inventory tracking software that aligns with your business needs. Keep in mind that features critical for small businesses might not be as relevant for larger organizations. Evaluate your operations, budget, and goals to choose a system that works best for you.

A robust inventory management system like QuickBooks can help you navigate the complexities of inventory tracking while positioning your business for sustained success.

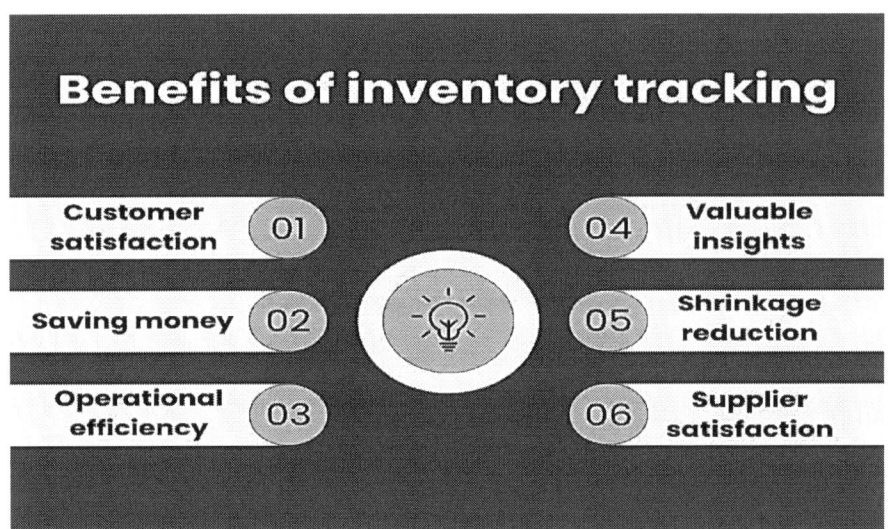

Benefits of inventory tracking

01	Customer satisfaction	04	Valuable insights
02	Saving money	05	Shrinkage reduction
03	Operational efficiency	06	Supplier satisfaction

To access inventory tracking features in QuickBooks Online, you'll need to subscribe to either the Plus or Advanced plan. If you're currently on a different plan, you'll need to upgrade to manage inventory within QuickBooks. Let's break down the key features of QuickBooks Online Inventory Management and how it helps streamline your inventory processes.

Key Features of QuickBooks Online Inventory Management

1. Track Stock in Real Time

QuickBooks automatically updates your inventory whenever you add stock or make a sale. This ensures you always know what's running low and what needs to be reordered.

2. Monitor Stock Value

Inventory values are updated in real time, keeping your balance sheet current and providing an accurate view of your stock's worth throughout the day.

3. Order Management

Stay organized with supplier orders. QuickBooks sends alerts when stock levels are low, helps you create purchase orders, and converts them into bills upon inventory arrival, ensuring timely payment tracking.

4. Organize Products

Group inventory items by adding pictures, product categories, or pricing details. You can also categorize items by tax status, making it easier to find and manage your inventory.

5. Automate Cost Calculations

Using the First-In-First-Out (FIFO) method, QuickBooks calculates the cost of goods sold automatically. This saves you time while ensuring accurate financial records.

6. Generate Detailed Reports

Access reports on best-selling items, total sales, and taxes. These insights help you make informed decisions and identify opportunities for business growth.

What Items Can You Track with QuickBooks Online?

QuickBooks Online Inventory Management enables you to track four main types of items:

1. Inventory Items

Track quantities of physical products you sell, whether you purchase them for resale (e.g., finished goods) or manufacture them from components (e.g., packaged products).

2. Non-Inventory Items

Manage items that aren't tracked by quantity, such as small components (e.g., screws for assembly) or items purchased for a specific project.

3. Services

Track professional services offered to customers, like landscaping, consulting, or repair services.

4. Bundles

Combine multiple products or services into a single package sold at a bundled price, making it easier to manage and sell grouped items.

Maximizing QuickBooks Online Inventory Management

QuickBooks Online Inventory Management offers a comprehensive set of tools to help you stay organized, streamline inventory tasks, and gain valuable insights into your business performance. By leveraging its features, you can optimize operations and focus on scaling your business with confidence.

How QuickBooks Online Inventory Tracking Can Help You and Limitations

Advantages

1. Easy to Use

QuickBooks Online is built with user-friendliness in mind, making it accessible even to those without an accounting background. The intuitive interface and guided setup allow for quick onboarding, while inventory tracking ensures smooth order fulfillment and efficient collaboration among team members.

2. Real-Time Inventory Updates

Inventory levels are automatically updated as sales, purchases, and transfers occur, ensuring you always have an accurate and up-to-date view of your stock.

3. Integrated Accounting and Inventory Management

QuickBooks Online combines inventory tracking with accounting, sales, production, and customer data management in one platform, simplifying workflows and improving manageability.

LIMITATIONS

1. No Support for Multiple Locations

QuickBooks Online cannot track inventory across multiple locations under a single subscription. Each location requires a separate subscription, and inventory transfers between locations are not supported. However, tracking for multiple warehouses is possible by creating separate item lists for each.

2. No Serial Number Tracking

QuickBooks Online does not support tracking inventory by serial numbers, which is often essential for quality control in manufacturing. For this feature, businesses may need to consider QuickBooks Desktop.

3. No Assembly Order Tracking

The software lacks the ability to track assembly orders, which is critical for businesses that manufacture products from raw materials or parts. This functionality is especially valuable for company's outsourcing components for finished goods.

How to Set Up QuickBooks Online Inventory Tracking

QuickBooks Online provides a straightforward five-step process to enable and configure inventory tracking.

Step 1: Enable Inventory Tracking

Before adding inventory, you must activate the inventory tracking feature. Follow these steps:

1. Navigate to Settings and select Account and Settings.

2. Go to the Sales tab and click Edit under Products and Services.

3. Check the box for Show Product/Service column on sales forms.

4. Ensure both Track quantity and price/rate and Track inventory quantity on hand are toggled ON.

5. Click Save, then select Done to confirm your changes.

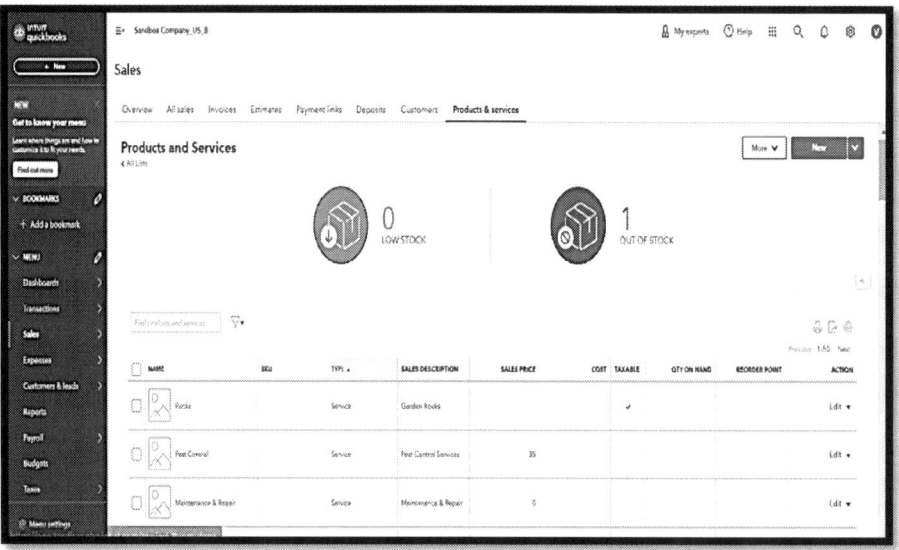

Step 2: Add Your Inventory Products

Once inventory tracking is enabled, you can start adding your inventory items along with other products and services you sell. Follow these steps to add an inventory item:

1. Navigate to Settings and select Products & Services.

2. Click New, then choose Inventory.

3. Enter the required details, such as the Name and SKU for the item.

4. Specify the Initial quantity on hand and set the "As of date" to reflect when you began tracking this item.

5. Set a Reorder point to get alerts when stock needs replenishment.

6. Under Inventory asset account, select Inventory Asset from the dropdown menu.

7. Provide a description of the product to be displayed on sales forms, like invoices or sales receipts.

8. Input the Sales price/rate and assign it to an Income account for tracking sales.

9. Adjust the Sales tax if necessary.

10. Enter the Purchase cost and assign it to the Cost of Goods Sold for the expense account.

11. Choose a preferred vendor if applicable.

12. Click Save and Close to finalize the entry.

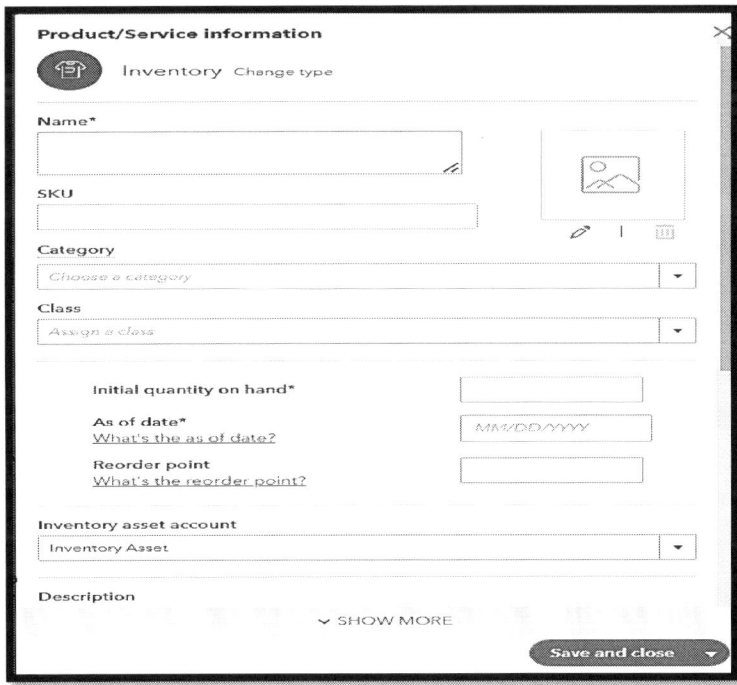

Step 3: Track What Sells

Once your inventory items are set up in QuickBooks Online, the software will automatically track them as sales occur. There are two ways to record sales:

- Creating Invoices
- Adding Sales Receipts

QuickBooks will update the quantity on hand for these transactions. Additionally, you can set a reorder point to receive alerts when stock is low.

Step 4: Restock Your Inventory

QuickBooks Online helps you efficiently manage inventory restocking. Follow these steps:

1. Go to Settings and select Products & Services.

2. Locate the product and click Edit in the Action column.

3. In the Reorder point field, enter the threshold quantity for reordering.

4. Click Save.

Once reorder points are established, QuickBooks notifies you when stock needs replenishing. You'll also have clear insights into what you receive from vendors.

Step 5: Use Reports to Monitor Inventory

QuickBooks Online provides detailed reports to help you stay on top of inventory management. These reports answer key questions, such as:

- What are your most popular items?
- What is the current quantity on hand?
- How much is the cost of goods sold?

To access these reports:

1. Go to Reports and select Standard.

2. Choose a report group like Sales and Customers or Expenses and Vendors.

3. Select the report that suits your needs.

These steps ensure effective inventory tracking while offering valuable insights into business performance.

Multi-Currency Transactions for Global Businesses

QuickBooks Multicurrency is ideal for businesses dealing with multiple currencies in their transactions. This feature allows you to assign specific currencies to various records, such as customers, vendors, or employees. It is particularly useful for:

- Paying vendors or employees in their local currencies.
- Receiving payments from customers or partners in foreign currencies.
- Managing foreign bank accounts in different currencies.

Note: Once the Multicurrency feature is enabled, it cannot be turned off. It may also limit the functionality of some other QuickBooks features.

KEY CAPABILITIES OF QUICKBOOKS MULTICURRENCY

The Multicurrency feature in QuickBooks provides several advantages:

- Make payments to vendors in their local currencies.
- Receive payments from customers and partners in foreign currencies.
- Automatically convert transactions to your home currency using current exchange rates.
- Deposit payments into bank accounts in a different currency.
- Pay employees in foreign currencies.
- Create customer accounts in specific foreign currencies.
- Assign foreign currencies to vendor accounts.

These features make QuickBooks Multicurrency an essential tool for businesses operating internationally or managing transactions across different currencies.

HOW TO SET UP MULTICURRENCY IN QUICKBOOKS

Before enabling the Multicurrency feature in QuickBooks, it's crucial to note that this action is permanent. Once activated, it cannot be disabled. Ensure you're prepared to manage multiple currencies before proceeding. Additionally, to safeguard your data, consider backing up your QuickBooks company file before enabling this feature.

Enabling Multicurrency in QuickBooks

The steps to set up Multicurrency vary between QuickBooks Online and QuickBooks Desktop. Below are the steps for QuickBooks Online:

How to Turn On Multicurrency in QuickBooks Online

1. Go to Settings > Account and Settings.

2. Click on Advanced.

3. In the Currency section, click Edit.

4. From the Home Currency dropdown, select your home currency.

5. Check the box for Multicurrency and confirm the prompt that it cannot be undone once enabled.

6. Click Save.

Adding Currencies in QuickBooks Online

After enabling Multicurrency, you can add the additional currencies your business requires. **Follow these steps:**

1. Go to Settings > Currencies.

2. Click Add Currency.

3. From the dropdown menu, choose the currency you want to add.

4. Click Add to complete the process.

Deleting Currencies in QuickBooks Online

If you no longer need a specific currency, you can delete it by following these steps:

1. Navigate to Settings > Currencies.

2. Locate the currency and click the small down arrow in the Action column. Select Delete.

3. Confirm by clicking Yes.

Once you've set up Multicurrency and added the necessary currencies, you can manage your multi-currency transactions seamlessly. For further details on handling these transactions, refer to QuickBooks Support for guidance.

Which Record Types Does QuickBooks Multicurrency Support?

QuickBooks Multicurrency feature supports the following record types, enabling businesses to handle transactions across various currencies:

- Customers
- Vendors
- Price Level Profiles
- Bank Accounts
- Credit Card Accounts
- Accounts Receivable
- Accounts Payable

In addition, QuickBooks users can utilize QuickBooks Payments for managing payments or integrate with third-party tools like Tipalti for advanced multicurrency payment processing. These integrations provide a broader range of payment methods and currency options tailored to the recipient's location.

Enhance QuickBooks Multicurrency with Add-On Integrations

For businesses looking for enhanced multicurrency features, integrating solutions like Tipalti with QuickBooks Online (Advanced, Plus, Essentials) or QuickBooks Desktop can provide:

Key Features of Tipalti Integration

1. Centralized Currency Management

Consolidate global payments without needing multiple regional bank accounts. Tipalti offers virtual accounts supporting over 30 currencies.

2. Convenient Currency Conversion

Automatically convert currencies for smooth international transactions.

3. Automated Payments

Simplify payment processes by automating transactions through Tipalti, reducing manual efforts.

4. Currency Volatility Management

Address fluctuations in exchange rates effectively with tools like Multi-FX and FX Hedging.

Benefits of Streamlining Global Payables

Integrating advanced payment systems with QuickBooks can streamline global payables processes, offering several advantages:

- **Time Savings:** Accelerate month-end processes by automating payables workflows.
- **Reduced Staffing Needs**: Avoid expanding your payables department as your business grows.
- **Decreased Fraud and Errors**: Automation minimizes the risk of payment fraud and human errors.
- **Cost-Efficiency:** Optimize cross-border payment processes, cutting down unnecessary expenses.
- **Real-Time Reconciliation**: Automate reconciliation for payments involving multiple currencies and methods.
- **Regulatory Compliance**: Ensure adherence to global payment regulations with robust tools.

Tipalti Multi-FX Benefits for Currency Conversion and Payments

Tipalti's Multi-FX functionality provides businesses with robust tools for handling foreign currency transactions, including:

1. Access to Real-Time Exchange Rates

Ensure up-to-date currency conversion for accurate financial management.

2. Visibility into Currency Conversions

Monitor the status of currency conversions easily.

3. Support for Over 30 Currencies

Facilitate payments in numerous international currencies.

4. Self-Service Transfers

Perform currency transfers directly within Tipalti for greater control.

5. Competitive Conversion Rates

Leverage Tipalti's transaction volume (over $43 billion annually) for better rates.

By integrating these solutions, businesses can optimize international financial operations and streamline global payment workflows.

CHAPTER 9
TROUBLESHOOTING AND SUPPORT

QuickBooks Online Accountant Troubleshooting Tips

When issues arise in QuickBooks Online Accountant, troubleshooting on your own can save time before contacting QuickBooks Support. The steps below can help identify and resolve problems or gather information to assist Support in finding a solution.

Initial Troubleshooting Steps

1. Clear Cache and Cookies: Remove any stored browser data that might be causing the issue.

2. System Requirements Check: Ensure your computer and operating system meet Intuit's system requirements.

3. Update Personal Information: Verify that your phone number and email in the Intuit Account Manager are accurate, especially if you're experiencing login problems.

If the issue persists after these steps, proceed with further troubleshooting.

User Troubleshooting Tips

1. Ask a Colleague to Try: Have someone else with the same permissions attempt the task.

2. Compare Settings: If they succeed and you don't, review and adjust your system settings to match theirs.

3. Consider Recent Changes: If the process worked previously, think about any recent changes in settings or software. Reverting to earlier settings might resolve the issue.

4. Look for Past Success: If you've never performed the task before, check if others in your team have done it successfully. Observe any differences in their approach.

5. Review Your Steps: Ensure you're following the correct sequence or have not missed any critical steps.

6. Try Alternative Methods: If possible, use a different method to complete the action and see if the issue persists.

These troubleshooting tips can help address common problems or provide helpful context for QuickBooks Support to assist you further.

System-Related Issues to Consider

Browser

- **Update Browser:** Ensure your browser is updated to the latest version.
- **Try a Different Browser:** Switch to an alternative browser like Chrome or Firefox.
- **Pop-Ups**: Confirm that pop-ups are enabled, and disable any pop-up blockers if needed.
- **Plug-Ins:** Verify that browser plug-ins (e.g., PDF viewers) are up to date.

Computer

Operating System Issues: If you encounter an error related to Windows or Mac, follow the provided instructions for resolution or contact Microsoft/Apple support.

Check for Updates: Confirm if your system requires any updates and complete them if necessary.

Network

Restart Modem/Router: Power off your modem or router, wait 10 minutes, and turn it back on to reset the connection.

Printer

- **Connection**: Ensure your printer is properly connected to your computer.
- **Update Drivers**: Check for and install any printer updates or driver patches.
- **Printer Settings:** Verify settings such as paper size and layout.
- **Test Printing**: Attempt to print from another website or program. If the issue persists, consult the printer manufacturer for troubleshooting.

Data Entry Troubleshooting

Check Entries: If a different value works, the original entry may have an issue.

Verify Data Accuracy: Confirm you're entering the correct data type (e.g., numbers for amounts, text for names) and avoid special characters that could cause errors.

Report Issues

If you're encountering problems with a report, review the following:

- Date Range: Ensure the date range is correct.
- Filters and Settings: Double-check any modified filters or display settings.
- Memorized Reports: Test whether the issue occurs with the standard version of the report.
- Transaction Accuracy: Inspect individual transactions for accuracy, as errors here might highlight the problem.

These steps can help identify and resolve common system-related challenges effectively.

Common Causes of Login Problems with QuickBooks Online

1. Incorrect Login Credentials:

The most frequent issue is entering the wrong username or password. Forgotten login details will prevent access.

2. Browser Compatibility Issues:

QuickBooks Online is designed to work with certain browsers. Using an outdated or unsupported browser can cause login problems.

3. Cache and Cookies:

Accumulated cache and cookies in your browser can interfere with the login process, leading to errors.

4. Internet Connectivity Issues:

A slow or unstable internet connection can disrupt the login process, causing delays or failures.

SOLUTIONS TO FIX QUICKBOOKS ONLINE LOGIN ISSUES

1. Verify Login Details:

Double-check your username and password for accuracy. If you've forgotten your password, use the "Forgot password" link to reset it.

2. Clear Cache and Cookies:

Clear your browser's cache and cookies to remove outdated or corrupted data that may block access.

3. Use a Supported Browser:

Ensure you're using a browser compatible with QuickBooks Online, such as Google Chrome, Mozilla Firefox, or Microsoft Edge.

4. Update Your Browser:

If you're using an older browser version, update it to the latest version for optimal performance and compatibility.

5. Check Internet Connection:

Ensure your internet connection is stable and fast enough to support QuickBooks Online. Poor connectivity can hinder login attempts.

6. Disable Browser Extensions:

Extensions or add-ons in your browser may conflict with QuickBooks Online. Temporarily disable them to check if they're causing the issue.

7. Contact QuickBooks Support:

If none of the above solutions resolve the issue, reach out to QuickBooks Support for further assistance. They can guide you through additional troubleshooting steps.

SOLVING COMMON QUICKBOOKS ISSUES

QuickBooks remains a favorite among small-scale businesses and accountants. This is quite understandable-the tool boasts a comprehensive set of capabilities with accounting task facilitation, besides the attractive pricing. Still, from time to time, an active user encounters errors within this system, usually related to poor training or unfamiliarity with some functions. Our guide is going to let you walk out of such typical QuickBooks error mistakes for smooth sailing with your QuickBooks.

COMPLICATED CHART OF ACCOUNTS

One common challenge in QuickBooks is dealing with a complicated chart of accounts. This typically happens when similar types of transactions or categories are assigned to different accounts, leading to confusion and errors in recording transactions. Fortunately, this issue is manageable.

HOW TO FIX IT

1. Resolve Duplicate Accounts:

QuickBooks doesn't allow merging accounts, but you can make duplicates inactive. For instance, if you have "Supplies" and "Medical Supplies," deactivate one and rename the other. Ensure you update past transactions to reflect the active account.

2. Remove Unnecessary Accounts:

If your business has undergone changes or you no longer offer certain products or services, deactivate accounts that are no longer relevant. QuickBooks won't let you delete accounts, but deactivating them keeps your chart of accounts tidy.

3. Label Accounts Clearly:

Use clear, descriptive names for accounts. For example, instead of "Miscellaneous Medical Supplies," use "Miscellaneous Supplies - Administrative Purposes" for clarity.

LOCKED DATA FILES

This issue arises when you try to move a file, perhaps for backup, and QuickBooks locks the file. You'll receive a pop-up notification preventing you from opening it.

How to Fix It

1. Update QuickBooks:

Locked files are often due to running an outdated QuickBooks version. Ensure you're using the latest version of the software.

2. Restart Your Computer:

If updating doesn't resolve the issue, restart your computer. Then, open QuickBooks by right-clicking the application and selecting "Run as Administrator."

ERROR 1317

This installation error commonly occurs in QuickBooks Desktop during software installation, preventing it from functioning properly.

How to Fix It

1. Use the QuickBooks Install Diagnostic Tool:

Download this tool from the official Intuit website. It automatically detects and fixes installation issues, including Error 1317.

2. Turn Off User Account Control (UAC) Temporarily:

UAC settings can sometimes conflict with QuickBooks installation. Temporarily disable UAC, then reinstall or update QuickBooks.

QuickBooks Won't Open Error

When QuickBooks refuses to open, it can be frustrating. However, this is a common issue with QuickBooks Online and is relatively easy to fix.

How to Fix QuickBooks Not Opening Error

1. Restart Your Computer:

simple restart can often resolve temporary glitches causing QuickBooks not to open.

2. Use the QuickBooks Tool Hub:

QuickBooks Tool Hub is a diagnostic utility designed to fix common errors. Install and run this tool to address issues that may be preventing the software from opening.

3. Run QuickBooks as an Administrator:

Right-click the QuickBooks icon and select "Run as Administrator." This helps resolve permission-related issues that might block QuickBooks from launching.

4. Update QuickBooks:

Ensure you're using the latest version of QuickBooks. If you're on an outdated version, uninstall it and reinstall the latest version to resolve bugs or compatibility issues.

ERROR 6000 OR 77

This error occurs when QuickBooks cannot access the company file due to incorrect file permissions, improper settings, or file damage. Thankfully, it's a fixable issue.

How to Resolve It

1. Check File Permissions:

Ensure the file you're trying to access has proper permissions. Modify the file's permissions to grant full access if necessary.

2. Run QuickBooks File Doctor:

Use the QuickBooks File Doctor tool to detect and repair issues related to error 6000 or 77. Download and install the tool, then follow the on-screen instructions to fix the error.

3. Relocate the Company File:

Moving the company file to a different folder on your system can sometimes solve the problem. Copy the file to a new location and try accessing it again.

Lost or No Connection to Data Files

Network problems can sometimes disrupt QuickBooks' connection to your data files. Although it might seem minor, this issue can prevent sending and receiving important data or invoices.

Steps to Troubleshoot QuickBooks Network and File Access Issues

1. Check Your Network Connection

Ensure that your network connection is stable and uninterrupted. Weak or intermittent connectivity can lead to issues when using QuickBooks.

2. Verify Firewall or Antivirus Settings

Firewalls or antivirus programs can sometimes block QuickBooks from accessing the network. Review these settings to ensure QuickBooks is not being restricted.

ERROR H202: UNABLE TO ACCESS COMPANY FILE

Description:

This error occurs when QuickBooks is unable to access a company file stored on another computer (host system). It usually arises from network configuration or connectivity problems.

How to Fix Error H202

1. Check Network Connection:

Confirm that both the workstation and the host computer are connected to the same network.

Ensure the network is stable and functional.

2. Adjust Host Computer Settings:

- On the host computer, open QuickBooks and go to the "File" menu.
- Select "Utilities" and ensure "Host Multi-User Access" is enabled. If not, enable it.

TIPS FOR RESOLVING QUICKBOOKS ERRORS

Having a basic understanding of QuickBooks and its common issues can save time and frustration. Identifying the root cause of an error is key to resolving it efficiently.

Common User Questions and Fixes

1. How can I fix mistakes in QuickBooks?

Errors are common in QuickBooks. Identify the specific problem and use tools like the QuickBooks Diagnostic Tool, which scans for and resolves errors automatically.

2. Why is QuickBooks not working?

QuickBooks might stop working due to update issues or file corruption. Updating to the latest version often resolves these problems.

3. What should I do if my reconciliation doesn't balance?

Recheck your records for missing information, such as uncleared checks. Adjust your balance to reflect any pending items until they are resolved.

4. How do I fix payroll errors in QuickBooks?

For payroll errors, such as sending an incorrect invoice, issue a corrected invoice and cancel the previous one to maintain accurate records.

5. How do I fix unrecoverable errors in QuickBooks Desktop?

These errors often occur due to corrupted data. Use the "Verify Data" utility to identify and resolve data integrity issues.

ACCESSING QUICKBOOKS DESKTOP ENTERPRISE SUPPORT

QuickBooks Desktop Enterprise provides access to professional support for technical issues, software setup, or advanced accounting tasks.

How to Get Help

Call Support: QuickBooks Desktop Enterprise Support can be reached at 1-866-347-6777.

Why Contact QuickBooks Support?

1. Technical Troubleshooting:

Address software errors, installation issues, or glitches quickly.

2. Product Setup Assistance:

Get help configuring QuickBooks Desktop Enterprise or upgrading from a previous version.

3. Feature Guidance:

Learn how to use advanced tools like custom reporting, payroll processing, and inventory management.

4. Data Recovery:

Recover lost or corrupted financial data to ensure business continuity.

5. Upgrades and Migration:

Ensure smooth data transfer during version upgrades without any loss.

QuickBooks Support is designed to help businesses overcome technical challenges and make the most of their software's features.

How to Reach QuickBooks Desktop Enterprise Support

If you need assistance with QuickBooks Desktop Enterprise, their support team offers multiple ways to help you resolve issues quickly. Below are the available options:

1. Phone Support

The fastest way to get help is by calling 1-866-347-6777. You'll be connected to a professional who can guide you through resolving your issue in real-time.

Tips for a Better Experience:

- Have your QuickBooks license number and business details ready?
- Be prepared to describe the issue clearly for quicker resolution.

2. Live Chat Support

For non-urgent issues or when you prefer not to call, live chat is available on the QuickBooks website. This option is useful if you're in a noisy environment or just prefer text communication.

Steps to Start a Live Chat:

1. Visit the QuickBooks Help Center on Intuit's website.

2. Select QuickBooks Desktop Enterprise from the product list.

3. Choose the Chat option to connect with an agent.

4. Share your issue during the chat; the agent may provide links or step-by-step solutions.

3. Submit an Online Support Request

For less urgent matters, you can submit a support request online. This allows you to provide detailed descriptions and attach screenshots or error messages to explain your issue.

How to Submit a Request:

1. Visit the QuickBooks Desktop Enterprise Support page.

2. Fill out the form with your contact information and a description of your issue.

3. Wait for a response via email or phone from a representative.

4. QuickBooks Community

The QuickBooks Community is an online forum where users, accountants, and experts share solutions to common problems. It's a great starting point for frequently asked questions or minor troubleshooting.

How to Use the Community:

- Visit the QuickBooks Community page.
- Search for topics related to your issue using the search bar.
- If no solution is found, post your question to receive advice from other users or QuickBooks ProAdvisors.

5. Social Media Support

Reach out to QuickBooks via their official social media channels, such as Twitter and Facebook. While ideal for general inquiries or updates, social media may not be suitable for resolving complex issues.

Tips for a Smooth Support Experience

1. Prepare Your Information

Gather details like your QuickBooks license number, software version, and any error messages.

2. Document the Problem

Note the steps leading to the issue and include screenshots or error codes for clarity.

3. Check the Help Menu First

Use QuickBooks' built-in Help menu for troubleshooting guides or articles related to your issue.

4. Contact During Off-Peak Hours

For non-urgent issues, call during quieter times to avoid long wait times, such as outside tax season or early mornings.

5. Request Additional Resources

Ask support agents for guides, tutorials, or tips that can help you manage QuickBooks more effectively.

Additional Support Resources

- **Help Center**: Visit the QuickBooks Support website for articles and video tutorials covering features and troubleshooting.
- **Certified ProAdvisors:** For specialized help, consult a QuickBooks ProAdvisor for setup, training, or advanced troubleshooting.
- **Video Tutorials**: Check the QuickBooks YouTube channel for videos on basic and advanced workflows.

When you need help with QuickBooks Desktop Enterprise, call 1-866-347-6777. Whether it's troubleshooting, setup, or expert guidance, the support team is ready to assist. You can also explore options like live chat, online forms, and community forums for additional support. Be prepared with the right information to make the most of these resources and ensure a seamless experience.

Backing Up Your Data for Peace of Mind

When using QuickBooks, it's important to understand which data can be backed up and which cannot. This ensures you're safeguarding essential information while managing expectations for what might need separate handling.

Data you can backup

Transaction data	List data	Other data
• Invoices • Estimates • Sales • Receipts • Payments • Deposits • Bills and bill payments • Credit notes • Supplier credits • Journal entries • Purchases and purchase orders • Refund receipts	• Accounts • Budgets • Classes • Currencies • Customers • Departments • Employees • Items • Payment methods • Tax agencies • VAT codes and VAT rates • Terms	• Attachments • Company Info • Entitlements • Exchange rates • Preferences • Intuit Payroll info backs up as journal entries • Stock shrinkage and adjustments back up as journal entries

What You Can't Restore from a QuickBooks Backup

QuickBooks backups include most essential business data, but certain information is not restored during the process. Here's an overview of what isn't covered and how to manage these gaps effectively:

1. Budgets

Budgets are not included in QuickBooks backups.

Solution: Export your budgets as a CSV file before restoring the backup to ensure you retain a record of them.

2. Stock Details

Stock history and adjustments are excluded from the backup.

Solution: Keep a manual record or re-enter stock details after restoring your backup.

3. VAT Rates (Expense Accounts)

If VAT rates are linked to expense accounts, they are restored as liability accounts instead.

Solution: Be prepared to review and adjust VAT rates after restoring to ensure they align with your previous setup.

4. Personal Cloud Archive Data

Data archived using personal cloud storage services, such as Google Drive, in a `.cab` format cannot be restored from a QuickBooks backup.

Solution: Manage this type of data directly through the cloud service you used for archiving.

HOW TO PREPARE FOR THESE BACKUP LIMITATIONS

To ensure a smooth restoration process, follow these steps:

- **Export Sensitive Data:** Save critical data like budgets and stock details separately before restoring a backup.
- **Use Specialized Tools**: Consider inventory management tools or cloud-specific backup apps for better tracking and retrieval.
- **Review Backup Files**: Check your backup for potential gaps and plan for manual adjustments where necessary.

Being aware of these limitations allows you to better prepare your backups and ensures no critical data is overlooked during restoration.

MANAGING BACKUPS IN QUICKBOOKS

QuickBooks has the most advanced tools to easily backup and restore your company data. Here's a simplified explanation of how you can manage your backups-whether you want to do it automatically or manually.

ENABLE THE ONLINE BACKUP AND RESTORE APP

With the Online Backup and Restore app, QuickBooks auto-saves changes to your data and dates those changes so that you can easily restore a specific backup at any time.

1. Go to Settings (gear icon).

2. Select Back up company.

3. Sign in with your Intuit account if prompted.

TURN OFF AUTOMATIC BACKUPS

To turn automatic backups off - if you no longer need them:

1. Sign in as an admin to the company you want to administer.

2. Go to Settings (gear icon) followed by Back up company.

3. Search for the company where you want automatic backups enabled.

4. Click the three-dot menu in the far-right Action column and choose Turn on Backup.

5. Type AGREE to confirm and choose Turn on Backup.

TURN ON AUTOMATIC BACKUPS

Need to re-enable automatic backups? Here's how:

1. Go to Settings (gear icon).

2. Select Back up company and sign in if needed.

3. Locate the company and click the three-dot menu under the Action column.

4. Choose Turn on Backup.

CREATE A ONE-TIME MANUAL BACKUP

Want to save your data instantly? You can also make a backup manually at any time:

1. In the Settings icon, select Back up company.

2. Add the company by selecting the Search for a company or firm dropdown and choosing the relevant business.

3. Click Next, then locate the company in the list.

4. In the Action column, click the three-dot menu, then select Run backup.

SAVE BACKUPS TO GOOGLE DRIVE

Linking QuickBooks with Google Drive allows saving backups to the cloud:

1. Go to Settings (gear icon) and select Back up company.

2. Open the User menu and choose Link Google Drive.

3. Follow the prompts to link your Google Drive account.

Note: It may take as long as 10 minutes for your backup to show up in Google Drive. You cannot, however, restore data saved this way via the Online Backup and Restore app.

CHAPTER 10

QUICKBOOKS ONLINE FOR ENTREPRENEURS AND BEYOND

As we approach 2025, the way businesses handle bookkeeping is evolving alongside technology. Intuit has announced that support for QuickBooks Desktop 2022 versions—including Pro, Premier, Mac, and Enterprise Solutions v22—will officially end after May 31, 2025. This shift underscores Intuit's focus on more advanced, cloud-based solutions.

If your business still uses these desktop products, now is the time to plan your transition to avoid disruptions. Switching to QuickBooks Online (QBO) offers a modern, streamlined solution for your accounting needs while simplifying your overall workflow.

Why Switch to QuickBooks Online?

1. User-Friendly Design

QuickBooks Online is designed with simplicity in mind, making it easy to use, even for those who aren't tech-savvy. If you're familiar with QuickBooks Desktop, the transition will be smooth, requiring minimal learning.

2. Flexible User Access

Unlike the Desktop version, QBO enables multiple users to log in simultaneously without needing extra licenses. This feature is ideal for collaboration, whether your team is in the office or working remotely.

3. Access Anytime, Anywhere

QBO lets you access your financial data from any device—desktop, laptop, tablet, or smartphone. Whether you're traveling, meeting with a client, or working from home, your company's numbers are always just a click away.

4. Hassle-Free Maintenance

Say goodbye to local data management, installations, and compatibility issues. QBO updates itself automatically, so you can focus on growing your business without worrying about troubleshooting software.

5. Enhanced Reporting

QBO offers advanced reporting tools not available in the Desktop versions. Customizable dashboards and detailed reports provide valuable insights into your business's financial health, empowering you to make informed strategic decisions—such as opening a new location or expanding operations.

6. Automation for Efficiency

Automation in QBO simplifies tasks like invoicing and expense tracking. These features reduce errors and save time, allowing you to focus on growing your business rather than managing repetitive accounting tasks.

WHAT ABOUT QUICKBOOKS DESKTOP ENTERPRISE?

For businesses that prefer to stick with a desktop solution, there's good news: QuickBooks Desktop Enterprise is still available. New customers can purchase Enterprise 24.0 subscriptions starting September 30, 2024, and current customers can renew their subscriptions without interruption.

While Intuit may eventually phase out Desktop Enterprise, it remains one of the most feature-rich desktop options for businesses that require advanced tools and capabilities.

Switching to QuickBooks Online is not just a shift in software; it's an upgrade to a more modern and efficient accounting solution. For those who prefer the desktop experience, Enterprise continues to provide robust functionality for your needs.

Future-Proof Your Accounting with QuickBooks Online

Intuit's decision to retire some Desktop products is a step toward cloud-based solutions that are flexible, accessible, and collaborative. QuickBooks Online is designed to meet the needs of modern businesses, helping you stay ahead with enhanced reporting, automation, and seamless user access.

Whether you are ready to make the transition or simply have questions about these changes, our team is ready to support you. We will be able to walk you through the process and make sure you find the perfect accounting solutions for your business, regardless of your industry.

SCALING YOUR BUSINESS WITH QUICKBOOKS ONLINE

As we journey deeper into 2025, e-invoicing remains in a state of metamorphosis. With constant change comes new trends and regulations that businesses, most especially

SMBs and accounting professionals, must keep in step with. Awareness of the latest changes is essential for efficiency, compliance, and competitiveness.

Here's an overview of what's shaping the e-invoicing world in 2025 and how you can prepare.

KEY E-INVOICING TRENDS FOR 2025

1. AI and Machine Learning Take the Lead

More Automation: AI-powered tools will take over more invoicing tasks like data extraction, validation, fraud detection, and error prevention, saving time and reducing mistakes.

Smarter Insights: Machine learning will provide businesses with predictions for cash flow, payment trends, and compliance alerts, helping make proactive decisions.

Tailored Invoicing: Businesses will be able to send personalized invoices, including customized payment options and communication methods based on customer preferences.

2. Blockchain for Secure and Transparent Transactions

Tamper-Proof Records: Blockchain technology ensures that invoices are stored as unchangeable records, enhancing trust and security.

Smart Contracts: These enable automated payments with triggers that ensure timely and accurate settlements.

Simplified Cross-Border Payments: Blockchain streamlines international invoicing by providing a single, efficient transaction platform.

3. CLOUD-BASED SOLUTIONS GAIN PROMINENCE

Access Anywhere: Cloud-based platforms allow businesses to manage invoices from any device, making hybrid work models more efficient.

Scalability: These platforms can grow with a business, handling increasing transaction volumes effortlessly.

Centralized Data: Real-time invoicing analytics offer better insights for informed business decisions.

4. Push for Interoperability and Standardization

Global Standards: Formats like UBL and PEPPOL are driving the standardization of cross-border invoicing processes, simplifying international transactions.

Improved APIs: Enhanced APIs allow seamless integration with ERP systems, ensuring smooth regulatory compliance and efficient data sharing.

5. Sustainability Takes the Spotlight

Paperless Processes: Environmental concerns will push more businesses toward fully digital invoicing, reducing paper use.

Green Compliance: Future regulations may require businesses to monitor and report their carbon footprint through electronic invoicing systems.

LEGAL UPDATES FOR 2025

1. E-Invoicing Becomes Mandatory in More Regions

B2G and B2B Compliance: Governments are increasingly requiring businesses of all sizes to adopt e-invoicing to ensure accurate tax declarations.

Uniform Standards: Standardized e-invoice formats aim to simplify accounting and tax filing procedures.

2. Real-Time Reporting Becomes Standard

Instant Validation: Tax invoices will be validated in real time, reducing errors and minimizing fraud risks.

Automated Tax Calculations: Automated systems will handle tax calculations to improve accuracy and efficiency.

3. Stricter Data Privacy and Protection Rules

Enhanced Security: Sensitive data will be protected with encryption, digital signatures, and stricter access controls.

Cross-Border Data Rules: Businesses will need to comply with global regulations regarding the transfer and storage of data across different regions.

4. Digital Identity Verification

KYC Requirements: Companies will be required to verify the identities of their partners before issuing e-invoices.

e-Signature Authentication: Digital signatures will be used to verify invoices and prevent unauthorized alterations.

5. International Cooperation Among Tax Authorities

Data Sharing: Tax authorities across countries will share data to detect fraud and promote global compliance.

Harmonized Regulations: Coordinated regulations will make it easier for companies to operate across borders.

HOW TO STAY AHEAD

1. Upgrade to Advanced E-Invoicing Systems

- Look for platforms with AI, blockchain, and cloud features that ensure compliance and efficiency.

2. Focus on Security

- Adopt encryption and secure access controls to protect your invoicing data. Regularly audit your systems to stay compliant with data protection laws.

3. Stay Up to Date and Agile:

- Keep abreast of all changes in regulations and market trends. Update your processes and systems accordingly to ensure compliance, but also leverage the benefit of new innovations.

4. Employee Education

Invest in teaching employees to be confident with new tools and rules. This will help all parties in your business get accustomed to new ways.

5. Engage Stakeholders

Work with your partners, customers, and regulators to ensure a seamless transition to modern e-invoicing.

By embracing the latest technology, prioritizing security, and being proactive about compliance, businesses can not only navigate the changing landscape of e-invoicing but also leverage it to boost efficiency and growth.

QUICKBOOKS BEST PRACTICES FOR LONG TERM SUCCESS

Every single industry has best practices, of course, but when it comes down to the wire, having decent accounting and bookkeeping provides the most essential backbone to running a business-be it equipment expenses for hospitals or complex multi-state sales tax for e-commerce.

By following these seven QuickBooks Online (QBO) strategies, you'll improve productivity, protect data integrity, and maintain accurate financial records—month after month, year after year.

Why Best Practices Are Essential

Adopting good accounting practices isn't just about keeping your books in order. It helps:

- Ensure your financial data is accurate.
- Save time by streamlining processes.
- Provide clear insights into your business's financial health.

Moreover, these practices build trust and strengthen relationships with customers and vendors. Professional, timely invoices and clear receipts demonstrate your commitment to quality and reliability.

QuickBooks Online Tips for Business Owners

1. Track 1099 Vendors

If you hire contractors, ensure their 1099 status is marked in QuickBooks. This simplifies tax compliance and makes generating and sending 1099 forms effortless.

2. Reconcile Regularly

Reconciliation is essential, not just a bookkeeping chore. Comparing downloaded transactions with your accounts helps identify errors, missing entries, or discrepancies, giving you a clear picture of your cash flow.

3. Clean Up Your Lists

Old records for products, services, customers, and vendors can clutter your data. Periodically mark inactive records to keep your QuickBooks file organized and easier to manage.

4. Categorize Transactions Properly

Properly categorizing income and expenses ensures accurate reporting. Use QuickBooks features like Classes, Categories, and Tags to organize transactions, helping you uncover trends for better decision-making.

5. Manage User Permissions

Protect your financial data by carefully assigning user permissions. Restrict access to sensitive areas like customer payment details or credit card information to only those who need it.

6. Use Built-In Reports

QuickBooks offers powerful reporting tools. Regularly review reports such as "Who Owes You" and "What You Owe." Generate financial statements like Profit and Loss or Cash Flow reports to gain a deeper understanding of your operations.

PRIORITIZE SECURITY

Ensure the security of your business data by:

- Logging off after every session.
- Avoiding public Wi-Fi while using the mobile app to minimize cyber threats.

The Bottom Line

By adopting these QuickBooks practices, you'll stay organized, safeguard your data, and gain valuable insights for smarter business decisions. Accurate data and secure systems not only improve financial health but also build long-term trust with customers and vendors.

The Future of Cloud Accounting with QuickBooks Online in 2025

QuickBooks cloud accounting software eliminates repetitive tasks, allowing you to focus on growing your business. Here's how it helps:

- **Track Income and Expenses:** Stay on top of your cash flow effortlessly.
- **GST and VAT Compliance**: Easily track and manage taxes, staying compliant with changing regulations.
- **Inventory Management**: Monitor stock levels and receive low-stock alerts.

- **Custom Recurring Invoices**: Automate invoice generation to suit your schedule.
- **Late Payment Reminders:** Automatically send reminders to encourage timely payments.
- **Payment Matching:** Quickly reconcile payments with transactions for accurate records.
- **Scheduled Reports**: Generate and share essential reports on time without hassle.

QuickBooks simplifies accounting so you can focus on what truly matters: growing your business.

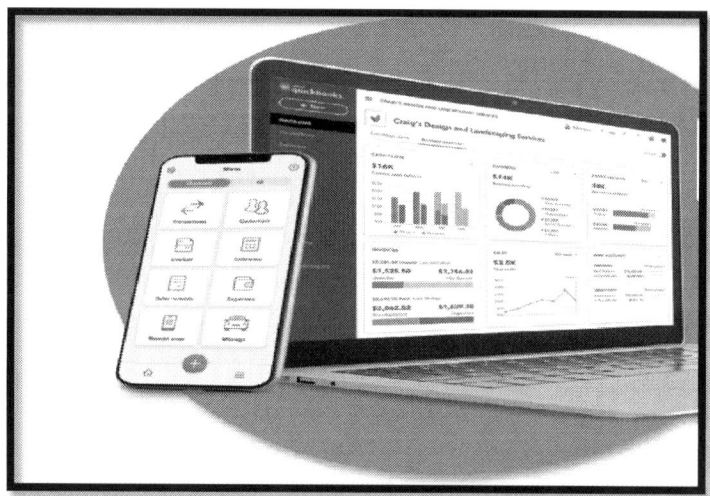

Get a Real-Time Snapshot of Your Business

QuickBooks cloud accounting software keeps you current with real-time financial insights. Instantly access your cash flow, bank balances, transactions, and financial reports to empower smarter and faster decisions for your business.

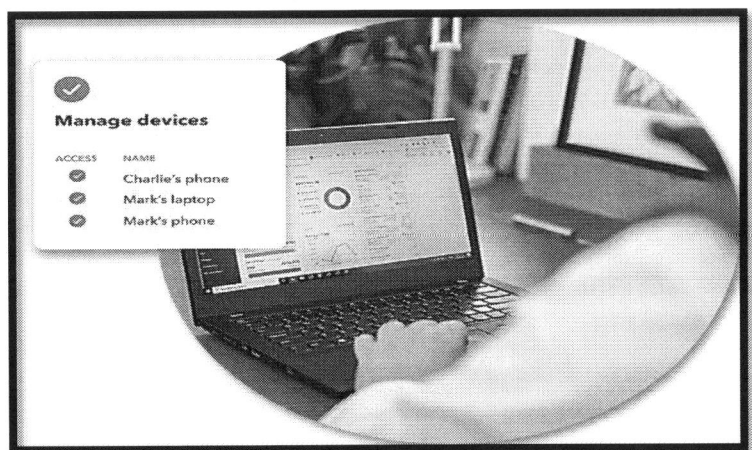

Easy Cloud-Based Collaboration

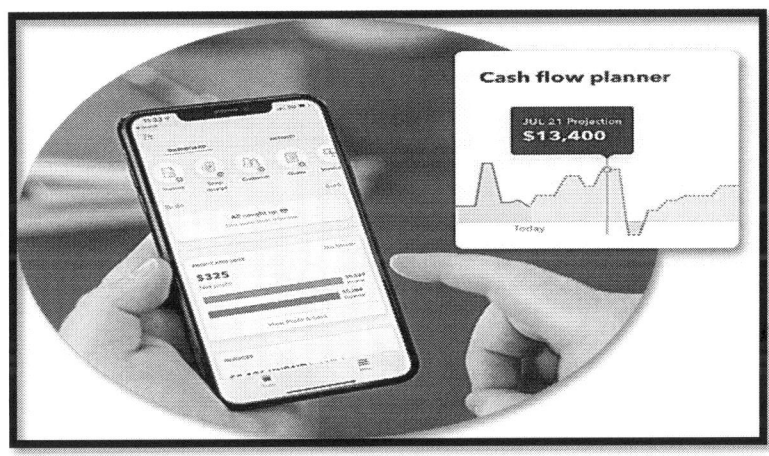

Simplify teamwork: Invite your accountant, bookkeeper, or employees to collaborate in the cloud. Click a few buttons and securely set or update access permissions so everyone's on the same page, yet your data stays under your control.

Simplified QuickBooks Year-End Tips for Business Owners and Accountants

QuickBooks Online is packed with tools designed to simplify your accounting and tax preparation process. Here's an easy-to-follow guide on its key features to help streamline your year-end financial tasks.

1. Auto-Categorization for Expenses

Save time with QuickBooks' automatic transaction categorization feature, which sorts expenses based on rules you set. You can review and tweak these categories to ensure tax compliance.

Steps to Use Auto-Categorization:

- Create rules by navigating to Banking > Rules, and set conditions by vendor or keyword.
- Review and confirm transactions under Banking > Categorize before finalizing.

2. Bank and Credit Card Reconciliation

QuickBooks' reconciliation tool matches transactions to your bank statement, ensuring accurate records.

How to Reconcile Accounts:

- Go to Accounting > Reconcile, select the account, and enter the statement's ending balance.
- Filter for unreconciled transactions and confirm matches.
- Ensure the Difference column shows a zero balance before completing the process.

3. QuickBooks Reports for Year-End Review

QuickBooks provides customizable reports that simplify financial reviews and tax preparation.

Key Reports to Run:

- **Profit and Loss**: Found under Reports > Profit & Loss, this report tracks income and expenses.
- **Balance Sheet:** Access it via Reports > Balance Sheet to see your assets versus liabilities.
- **Trial Balance**: Located under Reports > Accountant Reports, this ensures all accounts are balanced.

4. 1099 Tracking and Filing

QuickBooks makes contractor payment tracking and 1099 filing straightforward, reducing stress during tax season.

How to Set Up and File 1099s:

- Enable 1099 tracking for contractors by going to Expenses > Vendors and selecting Track payments for 1099.
- Prepare 1099 forms under Expenses > Vendors > Prepare 1099s, ensuring all classifications and details are accurate.

5. Accounts Receivable (A/R) Management

QuickBooks' batch invoicing and A/R tools help keep client payments and records organized.

Steps to Manage A/R:

- Review outstanding payments via the Open Invoices Report under Sales > Invoices.
- Simplify payments by batch invoicing in Sales > Customers.
- Highlight overdue accounts with the Accounts Receivable Aging Report in Reports > Accountant Reports.

6. Cash Flow Projections for 2025

Use QuickBooks' cash flow forecasting tool to help clients anticipate future income and expenses, ensuring better financial planning.

Steps to Create Cash Flow Projections:

- Set the income and expense projections under Dashboard > Business Overview > Cash Flow.
- Include any upcoming major expenses or changes in income for improved accuracy.
- Use the summarized data to guide budgeting and decision-making for Q1 2025.

By mastering these QuickBooks features, you'll streamline year-end tasks, ensure accurate financial records, and help your clients start the new year with confidence and clarity.

INDEX

A

Accessing QuickBooks Desktop Enterprise Support · 172
Adding Bills to QuickBooks · 90
Advanced Features for Growing Businesses · 148
automate Bookkeeping · 66
Automating Payroll Calculations and Tax Filing · 112
Automating Repetitive Tasks to Save Time · 64
Automation in Real-Time Accounting · 124
Avoiding Common Tax Filing Mistakes · 142

B

Backing Up Your Data for Peace of Mind · 175
Benefits of Payroll Automation · 113
bookkeeping · 1, 25, 29, 34, 37, 40, 42, 65, 67, 140, 179, 184

C

Choosing the Best QuickBooks Plan for Your Business · 38
Compatible Browsers for Tablets and Mobile Devices · 23

Completing the Details for a Recurring Template · 105
Creating and Customizing Professional Invoices · 73
CUSTOMIZING REPORTS TO FIT YOUR BUSINESS NEEDS · 129
CUSTOMIZING YOUR QUICKBOOKS ONLINE EXPERIENCE · 41

D

Deactivating an Account in QuickBooks Online · 58

E

EMBRACE THE FUTURE WITH QUICKBOOKS ONLINE 2025 · 1
Embracing the Future of Business Accounting · 2
Entering Vendor Payment Information in QuickBooks · 99
Essential Year-End Reports to Run · 7

F

Frequently Asked Questions · 63
Future-Proof Your Business with QuickBooks Online · 4

G

GET STARTED WITH QUICKBOOKS IN JUST A FEW MINUTES · 24

GETTING STARTED WITH QUICKBOOKS ONLINE · 13

Getting Started: Key Setup Tips · 45

H

How to Connect Credit Card Accounts to QuickBooks Online · 62

How to Create a Recurring Transaction · 103

How to Delete a Deposit in QuickBooks Online · 20

How to Stay Ahead · 183

How to Undo Reconciliation in QuickBooks Online · 19

How to Write a Payment Reminder Letter · 85

I

INVENTORY MANAGEMENT AND TRACKING MADE SIMPLE · 151

invoices · 8, 9, 11, 12, 16, 21, 24, 25, 26, 30, 31, 41, 45, 48, 50, 51, 65, 69, 72, 73, 74, 75, 76, 77, 78, 79, 80, 81, 84, 85, 100, 102, 138, 148, 150, 157, 170, 181, 182, 183, 184

K

Key Capabilities of QuickBooks Multicurrency · 159

Key E-Invoicing Trends for 2025 · 181

Key Features of QuickBooks Dashboards · 131

Key Features of QuickBooks Online Inventory Management · 153

L

Linking Your Bank and Credit Card Accounts Securely · 61

M

Make Your Invoices a Valuable Resource · 76

Managing Backups in QuickBooks · 177

Managing Benefits Bonuses and Contractor Payments · 119

MANAGING EXPENSES AND BILLS · 90

Managing Overdue Invoices and Client Follow-Ups · 84

MARKETING STRATEGIES THAT DRIVE QUICKBOOKS' SUCCESS · 135

Mastering Financial Basics · 44

Must-Have Tools and Updates in QuickBooks Online 2025 · 6

N

Navigating the Interface Like a Pro · 35

O

Overlooked Deductions and Credits · 145

P

Payroll and Employee Management Made Simple · 107
PREPARING FOR TAX TIME WITH QUICKBOOKS ONLINE · 139
Processing Payments in QuickBooks Online · 82

Q

Quick Start Checklist · 13
QuickBooks · 1, 2, 3, 4, 5, 6, 7, 8, 9, 10, 11, 12, 13, 14, 15, 16, 17, 18, 19, 20, 21, 22, 23, 24, 25, 26, 29, 30, 31, 32, 33, 34, 35, 36, 37, 38, 39, 40, 41, 42, 43, 44, 45, 46, 47, 50, 51, 52, 54, 57, 58, 60, 61, 62, 63, 64, 73, 74, 75, 76, 77, 78, 79, 80, 82, 86, 87, 88, 89, 90, 91, 92, 93, 94, 95, 96, 97, 98, 99, 101, 102, 103, 105, 106, 107, 108, 109, 110, 112, 113, 115, 116, 117, 118, 119, 120, 121, 126, 127, 128, 129, 131, 132, 133, 134, 135, 136, 137, 138, 139, 140, 141, 142, 148, 149, 150, 151, 152, 153, 154, 155, 156, 158, 159, 160, 161, 162, 163, 164, 165, 166, 167, 168, 169, 170, 171, 172, 173, 174, 175, 176, 177, 178, 179, 180, 184, 185, 186, 187, 188, 189
QuickBooks Best Practices for Long Term Success · 184
QuickBooks Features Built for HVAC Businesses · 150
QuickBooks Online · 6, 9, 91, 92, 180, 184

QuickBooks Online for Entrepreneurs and Beyond · 179

R

Real Time Financial Reporting · 122
Recording Expenses and Uploading Receipts in a Snap · 91

S

Scaling Your Business with QuickBooks Online · 180
Setting Payment Options on Individual Invoices · 81
Setting Up ACH Bank Transfers for Vendors · 101
Setting Up Online Payments for Faster Transactions · 80
Setting Up QuickBooks Online for Financial Success · 39
Setting Up Recurring Invoices in QuickBooks Online · 79
Setting Up Vendor Profiles for Seamless Payments · 97
Setting Up Your Business Chart of Accounts · 51
Simplify expense management · 49
Simplify Tax Season with Prep for Taxes · 140
Simplify Tax Season with QuickBooks Payroll · 18
Simplify Year-End Bookkeeping with QuickBooks Online · 6
Simplifying Your QuickBooks Online Chart Accounts with flye · 57

Solutions to Fix QuickBooks Online Login Issues · 165

Solving Common QuickBooks Issues · 166

Step 1: Upload Your Receipts and Bills · 92

Streamline your invoicing · 48

STREAMLINING INVOICING AND PAYMENTS · 71

Supported Browsers · 22

SYSTEM REQUIREMENTS - QUICKBOOKS ONLINE · 22

System-Related Issues to Consider · 164

T

Tax Season Simplified · 137

The Power of Instant Financial Reporting · 123

Tips for Resolving QuickBooks Errors · 171

Track invoice status · 50

Troubleshooting and Maintenance · 47

Troubleshooting and Support · 163

Turn Off Automatic Backups · 177

U

Unlocking the Power of QuickBooks Reports · 126

W

What Is Accounting Automation? · 65

What is Bookkeeping? · 67

Who This Book is For · 9

Why Choose Factorial for HR Management? · 110

Why Choose QuickBooks for U.S. Payroll? · 109

Why Integrate Payroll and HR? · 109

Why Integrate QuickBooks Time with Unrubble? · 117

Why QuickBooks Dashboards Matter to Business Owners · 132

Why QuickBooks Online? · 39

Why Use QuickBooks Reports? · 127

Why Use TaxCloud with QuickBooks Online? · 87

Made in the USA
Middletown, DE
02 July 2025

10038139R00115